C-47 SKYTRAIN

in action

By Larry Davis
Color By Don Greer
& Tom Tullis
Illustrated by Joe Sewell

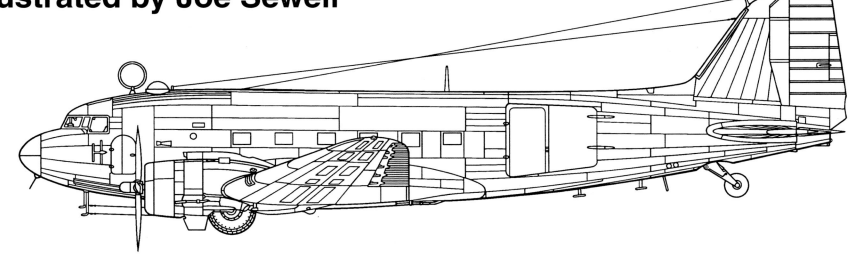

Aircraft Number 149

squadron/signal publications

CW00540057

C-47s of the 89th TCS, 438th TCG dodge German flak over France on the night of 5/6 June 1944. These C-47s carry Black and White D-Day stipes around the fuselage and wings.

ISBN 0-89747-329-0

If you have any photographs of aircraft, armor, soldiers or ships of any nation, particularly wartime snapshots, why not share them with us and help make Squadron/Signal's books all the more interesting and complete in the future. Any photograph sent to us will be copied and the original returned. The donor will be fully credited for any photos used. Please send them to

Squadron/Signal Publications, Inc.
1115 Crowley Drive.
Carrollton, TX 75011-5010 USA

軍用機、装甲車両、兵士、軍艦などの写真を所持しておられる方はいらっしゃいませんか？どの国のものでも結構です。作戦中に撮影されたものが特に良いのです。Squadron/Signal社の出版する刊行物において、このような写真は内容を一層充実し、興味深くすることができます。当方にお送り頂いた写真は、複写の後お返しいたします。出版物中に写真を使用した場合は、必ず提供者のお名前を明記させて頂きます。お写真は下記にご送付ください。

Squadron/Signal Publications, Inc.
1115 Crowley Drive.
Carrollton, TX 75011-5010 USA

Если у вас есть фотографии самолётов, вооружения, солдат или кораблей любой страны, особенно, снимки времён войны, поделитесь с нами и помогите сделать новые книги издательства Эскадрон/Сигнал ещё интереснее. Мы переснимем ваши фотографии и вернём оригиналы. Имена приславших снимки будут сопровождать все опубликованные фотографии. Пожалуйста, присылайте фотографии по адресу:

Squadron/Signal Publications, Inc.
1115 Crowley Drive.
Carrollton, TX 75011-5010 USA

Acknowledgements:

Don Garrett Jr.	Tom Hansen
Leo Kohn	Art Krieger
James F. Lansdale	Terry Love
Ron Mackay	William Peters
C. A. Shaw	John Stanaway
Hans-Heiri Stapfer	Jim Sullivan
Larry Sutherland	US Air Force
Nick Williams	Air Force Museum

Operation VITTLES was one of the high points of C-47 operations was during the Berlin Airlift. There are nine Military Air Transport Service (MATS) C-47s unloading supplies on the Tempelhof Airport ramp during 1948. (AFM)

3

Introduction

It has been known by a great many names, most of which were derogatory — but lovingly so. Dizzy Three, Dakota, Skytrain, Gooney Bird, Spooky, these are but a few of the many terms used to designate one of the world's most famous aircraft, the Douglas Commercial Transport. Technically it was designated DC-l, DC-2, or DC-3 as a civilian airliner type. But in the military it had no less than twenty-eight major variants. That's just counting the U.S. military types, without counting the many special types like gunships and electronic monitoring aircraft. The Douglas Commercial transport design, first brought forth during the early 1930s, has seen service with virtually every major nation on the planet, either as a civilian airliner or military transport. Although referred to in many terms, both in praise and derogatively, the Douglas DC-3/C-47 design is universally accepted as the plane that changed the world!

Donald W. Douglas Jr., founder of the Douglas Aircraft Company. (AFM)

The twin-engined Curtiss Condor bi-plane transport was considered one of the best airliners of its time, prior to the introduction of the Douglas DC-1. (AFM)

Donald W. Douglas Jr. was born on 6 April 1892 in Brooklyn, New York. Following the standard elementary and high school courses, Donald excelled enough to win an appointment to the U.S. Naval Academy at Annapolis in 1909. But after three years Douglas tired of the strictness of academy life and resigned. Douglas then enrolled in the prestigious Massachusetts Institute of Technology (MIT), completing the full four year course in just two years, his major being aeronautical engineering. Following graduation he went to work at MIT as a Graduate Engineer, until being hired by the Glenn L. Martin aircraft company as their Chief Engineer. During the First World War Douglas returned to the U.S. military with the U.S. Army where he served as an aviation engineer. With the end of the war in 1918, Douglas went back to the Martin Airplane Company, where he began work on the first really large aircraft for the Army Air Corps, the Martin MB-2 bomber.

But Donald Douglas longed to design and build aircraft that were of his own design, for his own company. In 1920 he left Martin to start living his own dreams. Douglas left for the Los Angeles area in the Spring of 1920. He had no factory, nor did he have any money to buy or rent a building for his dreams to develop. But his reputation and ideas had preceded him to the Los Angeles area. In California he met David Davis, a millionaire with a great desire to fly. Davis put up the money and Douglas put forth his ideas on aircraft. The initial result was a single engine biplane design called the CLOUDSTER. The CLOUDSTER could lift a payload that was equal to its own weight, something no other aircraft in the world could do at the time. The performance of the CLOUDSTER was impressive enough that the U.S. Navy Department awarded a contract to the fledgling Davis-Douglas Aircraft Company to build three military versions of the design which could carry and drop aerial torpedoes. The Navy contract bought Douglas enough money for him to buy an old motion picture studio in Santa Monica. By the mid-1920s, Douglas designs were well known in both the civil and military aircraft industry. Militarily, Douglas built such memorable aircraft as the Douglas World

The Douglas DC-1 revolutionized the airline industry when it was introduced during 1933. The DC-1 combined safety, speed and maintainability, along with passenger comfort for the first time. (AFM)

The main competition for the DC-1 was to have been the Boeing model 247, the first all-metal, low-wing monoplane in the airline industry. But Boeing's ties with United Airlines allowed the Douglas design to leap ahead in production. (Peter Bowers)

Cruiser for the Army Air Corps. The Army DWCs made the first around-the-world flight in 1924. In the civil arena, the Douglas M-1 Mailplane was the standard of the era and the U.S. Post Office bought no less than forty of the M-2/M-3/M-4 Mailplanes for the Air Mail Service.

It would; however, be the U.S. airline industry which would bring about "the plane that changed the world." By the late 1920s, a great many people were flying, not only in the U.S., but throughout the world. Airline companies were springing up everywhere. United Air Lines, Transcontinental and Western Airlines (TWA), and American Airlines all had major operations in the U.S. Most of the airlines flew trimotors, metal skinned aircraft like the Fokker F-10 series and Ford ATs, the standard of the industry at the time. These aircraft were basically wooden-framed aircraft based on First World War I technology, i.e., they were obsolete even before they made their first flight. They flew low and slow, and were a maintenance nightmare. Following the crash of a TWA Fokker F-10 that killed Knute Rockne, the legendary coach of the Notre Dame football team, all the major airline companies began the search for a newer, safer, and easier to maintain aircraft. Douglas Aircraft Company came up with a design that not only answered all the airline industry requests of the era, but became the standard airliner of the entire 1930s and 1940s throughout the world.

5

Development

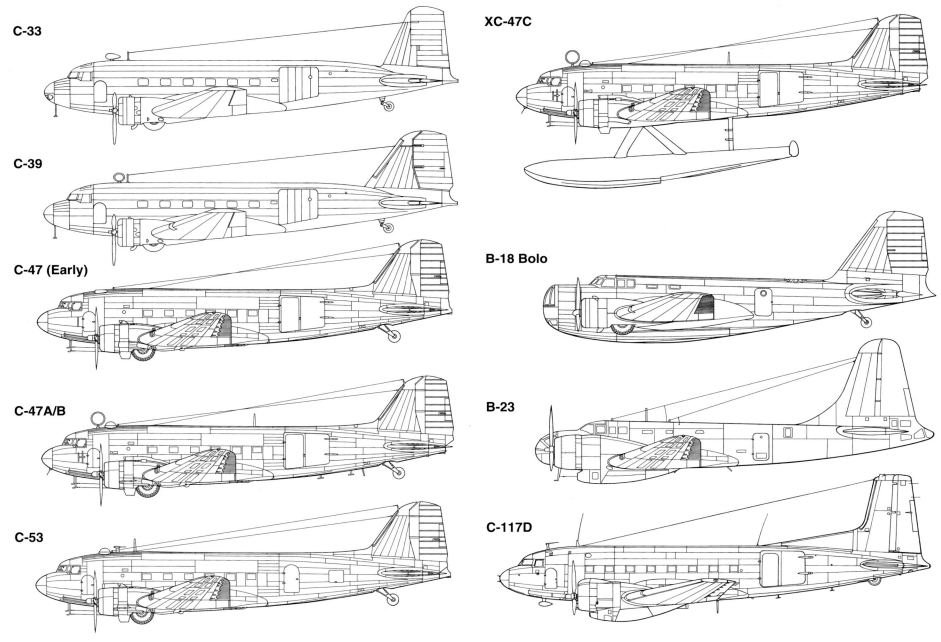

C-33

C-39

C-47 (Early)

C-47A/B

C-53

XC-47C

B-18 Bolo

B-23

C-117D

DC-1

The Douglas Commercial Type One, or DC-l, was the direct result of the growing maintenance problems throughout the airline industry. Maintenance that was required by the Bureau of Air Commerce (BAC), the forerunner of today's Federal Aviation Authority. The major airline companies decided that what they needed was an all new, safer and more maintainable design. Boeing had such a design in their all-metal, twin engine monoplane design — the Model 247. The Boeing 247 was the most modern aircraft of the era. United Airlines ordered sixty model 247s, virtually locking up the entire Boeing assembly line. All the other airline companies would have to wait until United's needs had been fulfilled before they could obtain any aircraft. TWA was not about to let the competition corner the market on modern air travel. TWA initiated a program to develop a modern airliner design of its own.

The TWA requirements were put forth to the aircraft industry on 2 August 1932, and it was very specific: an all-metal monoplane design, powered by three supercharged engines of at least 500 horsepower each, a crew of two and the capability to carry at least twelve passengers. The requirements also called for a range of at least 1,080 miles, with a top speed of at least 185 mph, a cruising speed of at least 146 mph, a rate of climb of 1,200 feet per minute, and a service ceiling of at least 10,000 feet. These were fairly normal requirements for the era. But the final TWA specification was not! The new design had to be capable of "a satisfactory takeoff under good control, after the loss of one engine while fully loaded, from any TWA airport!" These requirements were sent to all the major aircraft manufacturers except Boeing, including General Aviation, Martin, Consolidated, Curtiss and Douglas.

The Douglas design was easily the most advanced, and the most controversial. The fuselage was large enough for passengers to walk upright, a new innovation in the industry. And it was mated to a center wing/engine nacelle section for strength. The outer wing panels bolted to the center wing assembly, making for a much easier to maintain wing. The engines would be in the 700 horsepower range and would have full NACA cowlings for streamlining. But, and it was a very big BUT, the Douglas design would have only two engines. This meant the Douglas design would have to meet the TWA requirement of satisfactory takeoffs from any TWA airport after loss of an engine, on only one engine. Even the Douglas engineers feared they would not be able to meet this portion of the TWA requirements. TWA was; however,

The first DC-1 on the ramp at Wright Field during Army Air Corps tests in the Summer of 1933. Following its long career with TWA , the DC-1 was sold to the Spanish government and was destroyed in a crash during 1940. (AFM)

excited about the prospect and contracted for one airplane, it was designated the Douglas Commercial One, or DC-1.

The DC-1 rolled out from the Santa Monica, California assembly plant on 23 June 1933. It was bigger and sleeker than any other airliner design of the era, including the Boeing Model 247. The DC-1 carried only ten passengers in five rows of seats, split by an aisle way. But the DC-1 offered other innovations like a galley, a lavatory (for the first time aboard an airliner), sound proofing and cabin heaters. The two engines that powered the DC-1 were Wright SGR-1820-F air cooled radial engines rated at 690 horsepower each, turning Hamilton Standard three-bladed, variable pitch propellers. It would be these variable pitch propellers that proved to be the difference in meeting the TWA single engine takeoff specification. The DC-1 was sixty feet in length, had a wingspan of eighty-five feet, and had a height of sixteen feet. When fully loaded the DC-1 weighed in at 17,500 pounds. With the twin Wright Cyclone power plants, the DC-1 had a maximum speed of 210 mph and cruised at 190 mph, both well above the TWA requirement. The range was in excess of 1,008 miles and the service ceiling was an astounding 23,000 feet!

On 1 July 1933, Douglas test pilots Carl Cover and Fred Herman lifted the DC-1 off the runway at Clover Field for the first time. Minor teething problems with the carburetion system cut this first flight short, but all concerned were impressed with the aircraft. Following three months of extensive testing by the factory, TWA, and the BAC team, the DC-1 was granted a

The DC-1 prototype in full Transcontinental and Western Airlines livery on the ramp at Clover Field, California prior to its first flight on 1 July 1933. Carburetion problems with the Wright SGR-1828-F engines cut the first flight short, but not before the aircraft impressed all those in attendance, from both TWA and the Bureau of Air Commerce. (AFM)

U.S. Approval Type Certificate by the BAC. One of the tests the DC-1 was required to pass was, of course, the TWA single engine takeoff test. The flight test crew made a complete flight between Albuquerque, New Mexico (the highest point on the TWA route) and Winslow, Arizona — on one engine! TWA was more than satisfied with the test results and took delivery of the DC-1 in December of 1938. TWA paid $125,000 for the DC-1, although the proto-

The DC-1 had a passenger capacity of twelve in two rows of padded, single seats separated by an aisle down the center of the fuselage. Each seat had its own cabin window. (AFM)

(Above & Below) The overhead control panel and main instrument board of the DC-1. The aircraft was configured with an automobile-type control wheel. The center console contained the twin throttles, propeller controls and mixture controls. (AFM)

type cost Douglas $807,000 to build. But more importantly, TWA placed an initial order for twenty "improved" DC-1s that would have an additional row of seats. The "improved" DC-1 would be designated the DC-2.

Several changes occurred with the initial design as the DC-1 went through testing. The rudder/vertical tail assembly was increased in size for greater stability. A switch in engine types from Wright to Pratt and Whitney SD-G Hornets was tried, with the aircraft being redesignated DC-1A. Throughout its career, in both the military and civilian roles, the basic design could and would be ordered with either Wright or Pratt & Whitney power plants. The initial TWA design option was for Wright Cyclone power plants. TWA and Douglas used the DC-1 to set or break many U.S. and World Speed Records, including one trans-continental record of 3,107 miles at an average speed of over 272 mph. This "passenger plane" was flying rings around Army and Navy fighters of the era!

One of the most interested parties that tested the DC-1 was the U.S. military. The Army Air Corps had a need for a modern cargo/troop transport aircraft and the DC-1 seemed to fit the bill. In July of 1933. the DC-1 made a stop at Wright Field, home of the Army Air Development Center. Here, Army and Douglas test pilots put the big airliner through its paces. Although the Army liked the DC-1 design, they decided to wait for the "improved" aircraft before placing orders for their new cargo aircraft type. Following a full career, TWA sold the DC-1 to Mr. Howard Hughes. Hughes was going to race the DC-1. But it never came to be and Hughes sold the aircraft to the Spanish government. The DC-1 suffered an engine failure on takeoff from Malga Airport in December of 1940 and crashed. But the legacy of the DC-1 would live for decades, flying passengers, troops, and cargo throughout the world.

DC-2 Variants

The Douglas DC-2 was the follow-on aircraft to the DC-1, i.e., the "improved DC-1." The basic design was very similar to the DC-1, with two major exceptions. First there was a two foot increase in the length of the fuselage, bringing overall length to 61 feet 11 3/4 inches. Within the new, longer fuselage was the second change, an additional row of seats bringing total passenger capacity to fourteen. Other new features included stressed skin construction, wing flaps, a new rudder assembly and wheel brakes. The initial aircraft were powered by Wright SGR-1820-13 Cyclone engines rated at 875 hp for takeoff setting for maximum power. Based on the tests of the DC-1, and projected performance of the DC-2, TWA placed an order for twenty DC-2 aircraft. The DC-2 prototype, NC 13711, was rolled out in May of 1934 with the first flight coming on 11 May 1934. There were three major variants of the DC-2 built - DC-2 powered by Wright Cyclone engines, DC-2A powered by Pratt and Whitney SD-G Hornet engines, and two DC-2Bs powered by British Bristol Pegasus IV or VI engines.

The U.S. War Department was quite interested in the new Douglas transport design. The major transport aircraft type then in service was the Ford C-3/C-4 Trimotor and Fokker C-10, both types badly obsolete in comparison to the new Douglas design. The initial order for a military variant of the Douglas commercial design came, not from the Army, but from the Navy. This was strange considering the fact that Army Air Corps was the prime cargo mover for the War Department. The U.S. Navy took delivery of five DC-2 airliners, three for the Navy and two for the Marines, powered by Wright R-1820-10 Cyclone engines, designating the new type as R2D-1. All five were tasked as staff transport aircraft, the Navy assigning one each to Anacostia, Pensacola and San Diego. The Marine aircraft were assigned to VJ-6M at MCAS Quantico.

The Army Air Corps began development of the DC-2 series with the XC-32. Again, apart from military radios and instrumentation, the XC-32 was identical to a Wright Cyclone powered DC-2. The XC-32 was also used solely as a staff transport, and was based at Bolling Field, outside Washington DC, in 1935 for use by Pentagon brass. After the beginning of the Second World War, the War Department "impressed" twenty-four in-service DC-2 airliners for use in the Army Air Force. These "impressed", i.e., drafted, DC-2s were designated as C-

The XC-32 was the Army Air Corps version of the DC-2, and was virtually identical to the civil variant. It was used as the personal aircraft of General Andrews, Chief of the Army Air Corps during 1937. (AFM)

The "improved DC-1" was the DC-2. It differed from the DC-1 in being two feet longer to accommodate an additional row of seats. American Airlines specifications called for the passenger entry door on the right side. (Jack Binder)

32As. They were virtually unchanged from their role as civilian airliners except for military radio equipment. Indeed, many were "loaned" back to the airlines for service during the war, although usually not with the original airline that had purchased them.

C-33

The C-33 was the first of the type purposely built as a military transport aircraft. For the heavy cargo mission, Army had Douglas delete all the airliner furnishings and plush seating,

Fuselage Development

DC-2

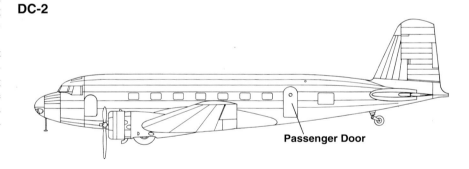

Passenger Door

C-33

ADF Bullet Antenna   Antenna Wire

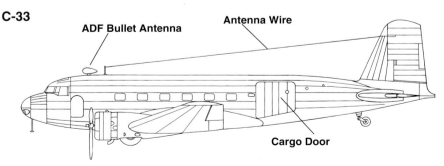

Cargo Door

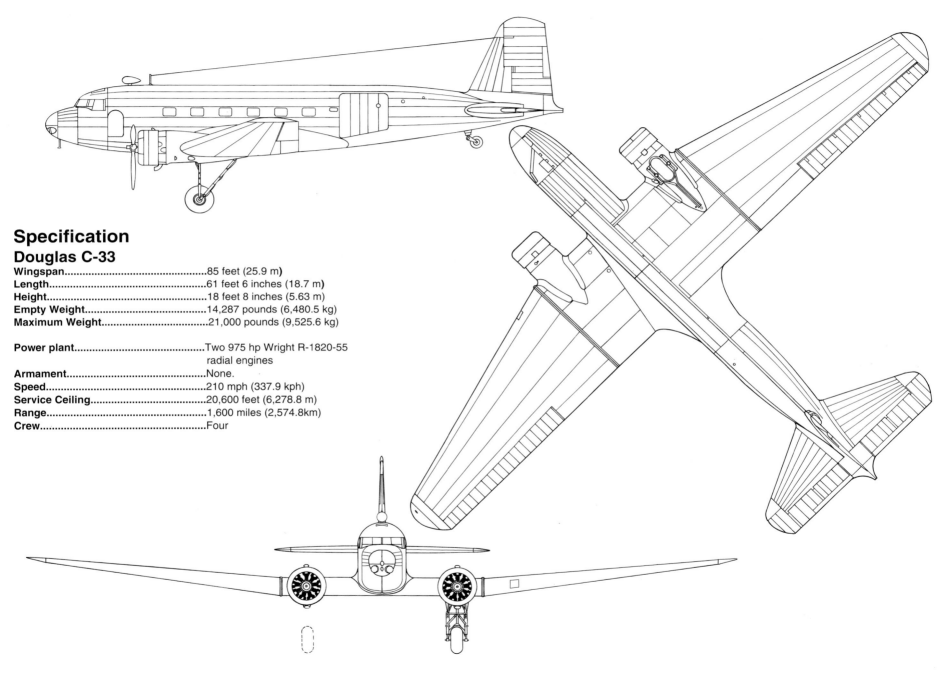

Specification
Douglas C-33

Wingspan.................................85 feet (25.9 m)
Length....................................61 feet 6 inches (18.7 m)
Height.....................................18 feet 8 inches (5.63 m)
Empty Weight.........................14,287 pounds (6,480.5 kg)
Maximum Weight....................21,000 pounds (9,525.6 kg)

Power plant.............................Two 975 hp Wright R-1820-55
                                                radial engines
Armament................................None.
Speed.....................................210 mph (337.9 kph)
Service Ceiling.......................20,600 feet (6,278.8 m)
Range.....................................1,600 miles (2,574.8km)
Crew.......................................Four

A pair of Army Air Corps C-33s share the ramp with some Army Boeing P-12 pursuit planes during 1934. The C-33 had a reinforced floor and a large cargo door on the left side of the rear fuselage. (Jack Binder)

The C-33 had landing lights mounted in the nose and the cowlings for the two Wright Cyclone air-cooled radial engines were very tight and streamlined. The aircraft carried a Direction Finder loop antenna on the upper fuselage spine along with a number of radio antenna masts. (AFM)

reinforce the entire passenger/cargo area floor, and cut a large door in the port side of the aircraft for cargo loading. The cargo door was split and opened barn-style forward. A cargo hoist could be attached directly to the fuselage above the cargo door. The door opening was over five feet high and almost six feet long. The C-33 could carry either twelve combat troops or over 2,400 pounds of cargo. As with the XC-32 and DC-2, the C-33 had a pair of military specified 750 horsepower Wright Cyclone R-1820-25 engines. Douglas built a total of eighteen C-33s.

C-34

The C-34 was a military version of the DC-2 similar to the XC-32 but with a fourteen seat passenger compartment. Two were built for use by the Secretary of War and operated by the 1st Staff Squadron at Bolling Field, outside Washington, DC.

C-39

The top of the line in the military DC-2 variants was the C-39. The prototype combined some features of both the DC-2 and DC-3. Douglas modified the first C-33 transport aircraft, serial 36-70, with the much larger vertical and horizontal tail surfaces of the DC-3. This solved the instability problem inherent to the DC-1/DC-2 series.

The C-39 took the modification a step further. The C-33 fuselage and outer wing panels were combined with a DC-3 center wing section/engine nacelle assembly, undercarriage, and tail assembly. The DC-3 vertical tail assembly later had a large dorsal fin fillet, similar to the C-47. The C-39 had the large cargo doors in the port fuselage, and was powered by a pair of

A C-33 transport shares the Langley Field ramp with a trio of Boeing P-12Cs and a Consolidated PB-2 during 1935. Douglas built a total of eighteen C-33s for the Army Air Corps. (Jack Binder)

975 hp Wright R-1820-55 Cyclone engines. With the increased power, the C-39 cargo payload was increased to 3,600 pounds. Douglas built thirty five C-39s for the Army Air Corps, with deliveries coming in 1939. Interestingly, the C-39 shared the assembly line with the much bigger DC-3. But no one in the War Department seemed interested in the bigger version of the Douglas transport until after the Japanese attack on Pearl Harbor. Then all the services wanted them — yesterday!

There were two final variants of the military DC-2, the C-41 and C-42. The C-41 was a staff transport that was based on the C-39, but used Pratt and Whitney R-1830 Twin Wasp engines for power. The Pratt and Whitney R-1830 Twin Wasp had 1,200 horsepower available in War Emergency setting. The C-41 did not have the large cargo door in the port fuselage. The single C-41 had a standard airliner passenger entry door on the rear portion of the port fuselage and was used by the Army Air Corps Chief of Staff, General Henry H. "Hap" Arnold.

The C-42 was another one-off aircraft built for use by GHQ Air Corps. It was identical to the C-41 except it was powered by 1,000 hp Wright Cyclone engines. During the war two additional C-39 transports were modified to C-42 standards and used as Staff and VIP transports. By the end of the DC-2 production run, Douglas had built a total of 193 DC-2s, fifty-eight of which were built to military specifications. Following the entry of the United States into the Second World War, the War Department "impressed" an additional twenty-four commercial DC-2s, for a grand total of eighty-two military DC-2 types.

(left) The cargo door of the C-33 was five feet tall and hinged forward. The door had two sections which could be opened separately. The aircraft had provisions for fitting the cargo hoist directly to the fuselage side. (Douglas Aircraft Co.)

A C-33 assigned to the Training School at Kelly Field, San Antonio, Texas during 1936. Most C-33s were retrofitted with the larger fin and rudder assembly of the C-39 to improve the aircraft's lateral stability. Only half of the fuselage cargo door is open. (Jack Binder)

A C-33 undergoes a 1,500 hours check at Hamilton Field during 1939. The Wright Cyclone R-1820-25 engines that powered the C-33 were rated at 750 horsepower. (AFM)

This Marine Corps R2D-1 was based at MCAS Quantico, Virginia during 1934. The R2D-1, built for the U.S. Navy, was the first actual military version of the Douglas DC-2 transport aircraft. (Bob Esposito)

13

A C-33 from the 63rd Transport Group unloads its cargo at Patterson Field during 1941. The football-shaped direction finder antenna replaced the older style open loop direction finder antenna. This aircraft crashed during 1943 and was totally destroyed. (USAF)

This C-33 carries the Olive Drab over Neutral Gray camouflage adopted by Army Air Corps just prior to the start of the Second World War. It also carries the pre-1942 style star insignia with the Red center. The serial number on the fin was in Yellow. (AFM)

The YC-34 was a military DC-2 with a capacity for fourteen passengers. It was quite plush for a military transport and used by the Army Air Corps to transport Very Important People (VIPs), such as the Secretary of War, during the late 1930s. The aircraft carries the Bolling Field insignia on the fuselage, just behind the placard holder for the Secretary's insignia. (Jack Binder)

The last DC-2 built ended its career in combat during the Spanish Civil War. It was used to fly spies into Spain during 1937/38. It carried the Spanish civil registration EC-AGN on the fuselage and wings, with just the country registration letters (EC) on the fin.

A C-39 assigned to the San Antonio Air Depot, San Antonio, Texas during 1940. One of the differences between the C-33 and the C-39 was that the landing lights were moved from the nose to the leading edges of the wing, giving the nose a much smoother contour. (Art Krieger)

The first C-39 on the grass at Wright Field, Dayton, Ohio during Army Air Corps testing in 1939. The C-39 combined a C-33 fuselage with the wing center section and tail assembly of the civil DC-3 transport. (AFM)

Fuselage Development

An overall Natural Metal DC-2 of the Royal Australian Air Force (RAAF) flies over New Guinea during 1941. The aircraft, RAAF serial A30-5, was an ex-Eastern Airlines DC-2, one of forty-five "impressed" DC-2s acquired by the British government under the Lend-Lease program. The aircraft carries the pre-war style RAAF insignia with the Red center dot. After the war began, the Red dot was quickly deleted. (AFM)

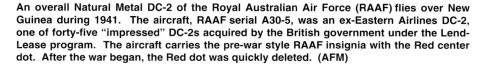

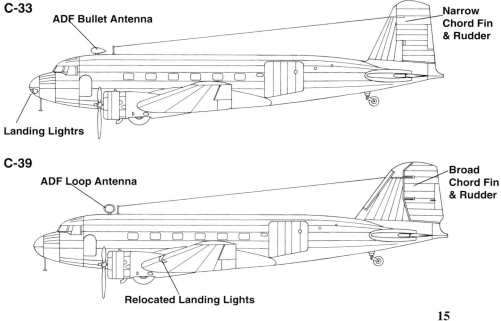

C-33

ADF Bullet Antenna

Narrow Chord Fin & Rudder

Landing Lightrs

C-39

ADF Loop Antenna

Broad Chord Fin & Rudder

Relocated Landing Lights

This C-39, aircraft number twenty of the 62nd Transport Group, was based at McClellan Field during 1941. Douglas built thirty-five C-39s during 1939, many of which shared the assembly line with the Douglas' next generation of transport aircraft, the DC-3. The aircraft was painted in camouflage during 1941. (Art Krieger)

This Royal Air Force DC-2 of No. 31 Squadron was based in Egypt during 1941. RAF DC-2s were all ex-U.S. airliners acquired under Lend-Lease. No. 31 Squadron camouflaged their DC-2s in a Dark Earth and Middlestone uppersurface scheme over Azure Blue undersurfaces. (Gordon Swanborough)

An Army Air Force C-39 delivers supplies at Seven Mile Airdrome on New Guinea during August of 1942. The C-39 served on all fronts during the war, until they were replaced by the newer and more capable C-47 Skytrain aircraft. (AFM)

The Douglas Bombers

By the mid-1930s the U.S. War Department had reluctantly come to the conclusion that the airplane would probably be *the* weapon for the next war, Billy Mitchell's sinking of the German battleship OSTFRIESLAND in 1921, using aerial bombs, burst the Navy's bubble that they alone could defend the United States from attack. America badly needed modern military aircraft to counter the growing threats in both Europe and Asia,

During 1934 the Army Air Corps issued a new set of requirements for the next generation of bomber aircraft. The specifications included a 2,000 pound bomb load, a range of not less than 1,020 miles (double this minimum if possible), and a top speed in excess of 200 mph. These specifications were almost identical to those issued by TWA for their first "modern" airliner type. The requirements were formidable enough, but the final requirement was that a prototype aircraft be ready for testing by August of 1935. Three companies had bids that would be ready to compete against each other at the 1935 Bomber Trials held at Wright Field, Ohio. The Martin Company had the B-12, an improved version of the B-10 then in service in the Army Air Corps; Boeing had the radical four-engined Model 217 (YB-17), and Douglas went with a bomber version of their very successful DC-2 civilian airliner.

The Douglas design, known as the Douglas Bomber type One, or DB-1, retained much of its airliner ancestry. The wings, landing gear, and tail assembly came almost directly from the C-39 military transport. The wingspan was increased due to a rounding of the wingtips. The tail assembly was larger in all aspects than that found on the transport and had the later DC-3 style vertical fin. The DB-1 was powered by a pair of 850 horsepower Wright R-1820-G5 radial engines.

But the major difference was, of course, a totally redesigned, much deeper and fatter fuselage. The DB-1 had a completely enclosed bomb bay nestled between the wings, which was capable of holding up to 4,408 pounds of bombs. The DB-1 had a crew of six: pilot, co-pilot, bombardier/navigator, and three gunners. There was a manual, rotating turret in the nose above the bombardier's station, a "pop-up" manual turret on top the rear fuselage, and a tun-

Fuselage Development

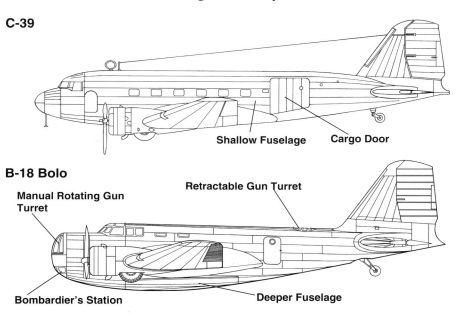

C-39

Shallow Fuselage — Cargo Door

B-18 Bolo

Retractable Gun Turret

Manual Rotating Gun Turret

Bombardier's Station — Deeper Fuselage

nel gun position on the underside of the rear fuselage. All three positions mounted single .30 caliber machine guns, which was the standard armament of the era.

The DB-1 was completed in April of 1935, allowing ample time to work out the bugs before the Bomber Trials in August. The DB-l was everything that Douglas and the Army had hoped for. The pay load was 4,400 pounds, the top speed was 233 mph, cruising speed was 173 mph,

The DB-2 prototype on the ramp at Wright Field in the 1935 Bomber Trials showing the powered nose turret and redesigned bombardier station. The standard armament consisted of single .30 caliber machine guns in all gun positions. (AFM)

The Douglas DB-1 prototype at Wright Field, Dayton, Ohio during August of 1935. The DB-1 combined a DC-2 wing with a new fuselage that carried bombs instead of cargo. (AFM)

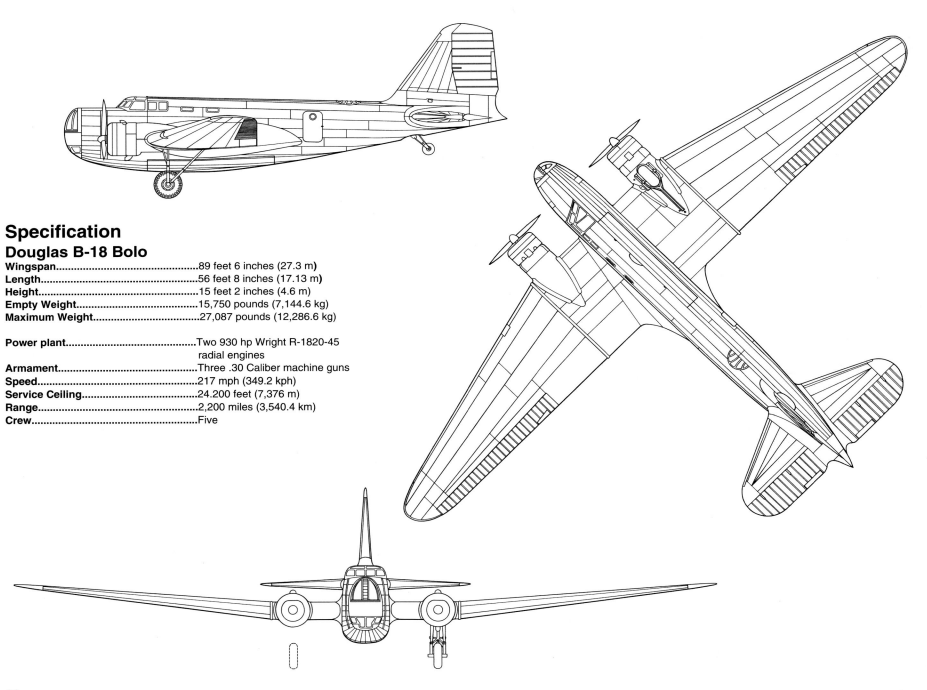

Specification
Douglas B-18 Bolo
Wingspan...89 feet 6 inches (27.3 m**)**
Length...56 feet 8 inches (17.13 m**)**
Height..15 feet 2 inches (4.6 m)
Empty Weight..15,750 pounds (7,144.6 kg)
Maximum Weight...................................27,087 pounds (12,286.6 kg)

Power plant..Two 930 hp Wright R-1820-45
                           radial engines
Armament...Three .30 Caliber machine guns
Speed..217 mph (349.2 kph)
Service Ceiling......................................24.200 feet (7,376 m)
Range..2,200 miles (3,540.4 km)
Crew..Five

A production B-18 Bolo on the ramp at Floyd Bennett Field during 1937. The production B-18 was virtually identical to the DB-1 prototype. The B-18 began coming off the Douglas assembly line in early 1937. The dorsal gun turret was fully retractable and housed a single .30 caliber machine gun. (Vincent Berinati & AFM)

The main instrument panel of the B-18 was very similar to the standard DC-2/C-33 instrument panel. The aircraft retained the automobile type control wheels used on the Douglas transports. The center console contained the engine and propeller controls. (AFM)

Ground crewmen perform routine maintenance on the engine of a B-18 Bolo. The nose area of the B-18 had a very distinctive shape with its gun turret and lower bombardier's station. The Wright Cyclone radial engines drove three blade propellers equipped with spinners. (AFM)

19

A B-18 from the 5th Bombardment Group (Medium) parked in the dirt at a forward airstrip in Hawaii during 1939. The overall Natural Metal B-18 carries typical Army Air Corps markings for the era, with Red engine cowlings. (AFM)

B-18s from the 88th Reconnaissance Squadron at Hamilton Field. Three Army Air Corps units had a reconnaissance mission and all were equipped with B-18 aircraft. The engine cowlings and command stripes on the rear fuselage were Black and Yellow checks. (AFM)

range was 1,030 miles with the specified 2,000 pound bomb load, and the DB-1 had a service ceiling of over 25,000 feet. But the Boeing Model 200 literally flew rings around both the DB-1 and the B-12. The Boeing design was much faster, more heavily armed and had a greater range. Only an unfortunate accident that set the Boeing program back almost a full year put the Douglas DB-1 into the forefront of the modern bomber picture. The Army declared the Douglas design the winner of the 1935 Bomber Trials and in January of 1936 ordered one hundred thirty-three DB-1s under the Army designation of B-18 Bolo.

The production B-18 Bolo differed little from the DB-1 prototype. The nose was slightly redesigned to incorporate a bomb aiming window. The engines were changed to Wright R-1820-45S rated at 930 horsepower. With full military equipment, the performance of the production B-18 fell off slightly; top speed was down to 217 mph, cruising speed was 167 mph, and combat range fell to 850 miles. But it was still the most modern bomber design then in

production. The first of a total of 131 production B-18s was delivered to the Army Air Corps in February of 1937. The original DB-1 was brought up to B-18 production standards and delivered to the Army. The final B-18 off the Santa Monica assembly line was built with a power-operated nose turret and a redesigned bombardier station. It was designated DB-2, but eventually it was returned to B-18 production standards.

There were many B-18s still in active service when the war broke out and they were rapidly given camouflage paint schemes of Olive Drab with Medium Green splotches on the flying surfaces and Neutral Gray undersurfaces. The serial number on the fin was in Yellow. The national insignia is the type that came into use during 1942, with the Red center dot being deleted. (J.N. Taylor)

This B-18 from the 7th Bombardment Group was based at Hamilton Field and carries the experimental water-based camouflage paint applied for the 1938 Army War Games. The colors were Dark Green, Olive Drab, and Neutral Gray, with Black undersides and Red cowlings. (AFM)

Fuselage Development

B-18 Bolo

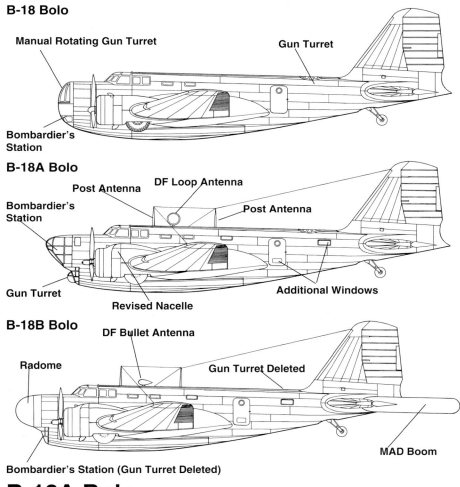

Manual Rotating Gun Turret

Gun Turret

Bombardier's Station

B-18A Bolo

Post Antenna

DF Loop Antenna

Post Antenna

Bombardier's Station

Gun Turret

Revised Nacelle

Additional Windows

B-18B Bolo

DF Bullet Antenna

Radome

Gun Turret Deleted

MAD Boom

Bombardier's Station (Gun Turret Deleted)

B-18A Bolo

The B-18A differed from the initial production aircraft in two areas, the nose and the engines. The engines were replaced by Wright R-1820-53S rated at 1,000 horsepower, and having full-feathering propellers. The entire fuselage forward of the windscreen was extensively redesigned with a distinctive shark-like appearance to the nose. The bombardier station was moved high into the nose in a large framed Plex-i-Glas fairing, that had the bomb-aiming window on the underside. Behind and below the bomb-aiming window was a small rail-shaped gun turret. The armament and other features remained the same as on the B-18. Army contracted for two hundred seventeen B-18As, incorporating them into the same units that

The B-18A had a totally redesigned forward fuselage with the gun turret relocated under the bombardier's station, giving the aircraft a shark-like nose profile. (Jack Binder)

A B-18A of the 19th Bombardment Group in flight over the California countryside showing the DC-3 wings and tail surfaces that were mated to the bomber fuselage to produce the B-18. (AFM)

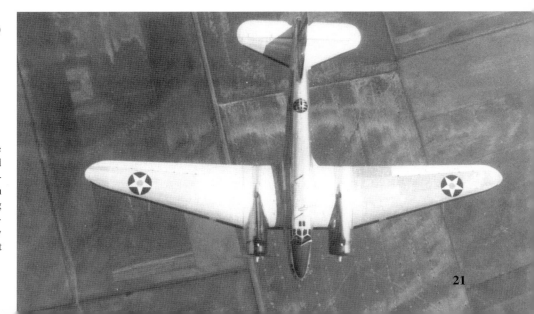

21

These B-18As were equipped with cameras and assigned to the 88th Reconnaissance Squadron at Hamilton Field, California during early 1939. The B-18 and B-18A were the Army Air Corps' long range reconnaissance aircraft until the B-17 went into production. (AFM)

B-18As of the 30th Bombardment Squadron lined up on the ramp at March Field, California during 1939. Douglas built 217 B-18As, these served alongside the earlier B-18 aircraft often in the same combat units. (AFM)

were equipped with the earlier B-18. The first flight of a B-18A came on 15 April 1938, with deliveries to the combat units commencing in June of the same year.

Digby Mk 1

The Royal Canadian Air Force purchased twenty B-18As in 1939 for use as maritime, anti-submarine patrol aircraft. These aircraft were designated Digby Mk 1s and differed from their U.S. Army Air Corps counterparts only in armament and radio equipment. The Digby Mk Is having Vickers .303 inch machine guns in the turrets rather than the U.S. Browning .30 cal-

A B-18A on the ramp at Albrook Field in the Panama Canal Zone during early 1942. The Howard-based B-18A flew Sea-Search patrols watching for German U-boats that patrolled the Caribbean Sea. (AFM)

iber machine guns. The twenty Digby Mk Is were delivered to the RCAF in late 1939/early 1940, and were assigned to No 10 (BR) Squadron, where they patrolled the North Atlantic in search of the German U-boats.

B-18B

Of the two hundred seventeen B-18As delivered to Army Air Corps, one hundred twenty-two were modified to B-18B standards to meet a specific need - the German submarine threat. German U-boats roamed up and down the Atlantic and Caribbean coastlines at will during the dark days of 1941/1942. The Army needed an airplane with modern submarine location/detection equipment, and they couldn't pull B-17 and B-24 aircraft from their production lines. The Douglas B-18A Bolo was, on the other hand, available in numbers. The B-18B had a great many changes dictated by the new mission of anti-submarine patrol aircraft. The entire bombardier shark-nose glazed area was removed and replaced with a large bulbous radome that housed a SCR-517 ASV (Air to Surface Vessel) radar. The bombardier's station

Twenty B-18As were obtained by the Royal Canadian Air Force (RCAF) during 1939 and designated Digby Mk I. The RCAF Digbys flew anti-submarine/maritime patrols over the North Atlantic during the early war years until replaced by Consolidated B-24 Liberators. (AFM)

A B-18B on patrol over the Caribbean Sea during December of 1942. The B-18B had the nose turret replaced with an air-to-surface radar, with a Magnetic Anomaly Detector (MAD) system in the distinctive tail boom. The B-18Bs were armed with depth charges to attack any U-boats they encountered. (USAF)

was moved below and behind the radome.

The tail was modified with the addition of a Magnetic Anomaly Detector system, or MAD, that was housed in a long tubular/boom behind and below the rudder, Additionally, the B-18B had long range navigational equipment aboard, and some airplanes had additional underwing racks which increased the amount of bombs and/or depth charges the B-18B could carry. Although the aircraft were rapidly modified and put into service at bases throughout the Caribbean area, they were even more rapidly replaced when Consolidated B-24s, with much greater range and bomb loads, became available in quantity.

The first operational B-18Bs were delivered to the 7th Bombardment Group at Hamilton

This war weary B-18B, (serial 37-543) had two U-Boat kill markings under the cockpit. The aircraft was camouflaged in the Sea Search scheme of Neutral Gray and White. (Leo Kohn)

Field, California, in the Spring of 1937. By the end of the initial production run, the Army Air Corps had three bomb groups equipped with B-18 Bolos, the 5th, 7th, and 19th Bombardment Groups; plus three reconnaissance squadrons outfitted with camera equipped B-18s. When the war broke out in December of 1941, there were still a great many B-18/B-18A aircraft in service, including some twenty-three aircraft assigned to the 5th and 11th Bombardment Groups at Hickam Field, Hawaii. Most of these were destroyed on the ground during the Japanese attack. Only the B-18B anti-submarine variant soldiered on as the B-18/B-18As were rapidly replaced with more modern aircraft like the B-17, B-24 and B-25. B-18Bs equipped several of the newly designated Sea Search Attack Squadrons, flying anti-submarine patrols from bases in the Panama Canal Zone. The last B-18B sorties were flown in August of 1943, at which time the unit was converted to B-24s.

There were two other variants or modifications in the B-18 series. The B-18AM was a designation given to twenty-two B-18s and nineteen B-18A aircraft that had the type D-3 and type B-7 bomb shackles removed, so that they could carry heavier ordnance. Finally, two B-18As had all their offensive and defensive armament systems removed and were used as transport aircraft. These were designated as C-58s by the Army Air Force.

Following the end of the war, several B-18/B-18A/B-18B aircraft were sold to private contractors such as SkySpray and used for such things as crop dusting or as plush VIP passenger transports. (Leo Kohn)

B-23 Dragon

Douglas followed the B-18 series with development of the B-23, nicknamed the Dragon. Whereas the B-18 was a development of the DC-2 airframe, the B-23 was based on DC-3 technology. The B-23 used the outer wings and landing gear of the DC-3/C-47. But the main landing gear was now covered by a full set of clamshell type doors, and the tail wheel was fully retractable, all in the name of streamlining and speed. Power was vastly increased over either the B-18 or DC-3/C-47, as the B-23 had a pair of 1,600 horsepower Wright R-2600-3 engines. The fuselage was totally redesigned with a slender, more squared cross section, a round bombardier Plex-i-Glas nose, and a much larger vertical tail.

The B-23 pioneered one feature that would be found on all subsequent bomber aircraft types through the Douglas B-66 jet bomber. It had a tail gun installation, the first bomber aircraft to be so equipped. A single held held .50 caliber Browning M-2 machine gun was installed in a streamlined tail fairing directly in front of the tail gunners compartment. The fairing was actually a pair of doors that opened to allow the tail gunner to traverse the .50 caliber weapon. In addition to the tail gun, a single .30 caliber machine gun could be fitted through a ball socket mount in the bombardier nose, another single .30 was mounted on a swing mount amidships, so that the waist gunner was able to fire through either open waist window position. And one more .30 could be fired through a ventral hatch to protect against attack from below. All these features were later found on combat B-17s and B-24s.

No actual "new" contract was let by the Army Air Corps for the B-23, with the thirty-eight production aircraft being substituted as a "change" in the B-18A production run. The first B-23 was rolled out from Santa Monica in early July 1939, with the first flight coming on 27 July.

Performance was considerably better than the best any B-18 type could offer. The top speed for the B-23 was 282 mph, with a cruise speed of 210 mph, which almost equaled the B-18s top speed. The service ceiling rose to well over 31,000 feet. While the combat range was greatly increased to 1,400 miles, the ferry range or maximum range jumped to 2,750 miles. The B-23 was fast, long-legged, and reasonably well-armed for the era. But not nearly enough in any area to equal the performance of either the B-17 or B-24.

The B-23 went into Army Air Corps service when four aircraft arrived at March Field California in 1940. March Field was home base for the 89th Reconnaissance Squadron, the

The B-23 Dragon was a further development of the B-18 series, with a totally redesigned fuselage and more powerful engines. The B-23 was the first Army aircraft to be designed with a factory installed tail gun position. (AFM)

Fuselage Development

B-18 Bolo

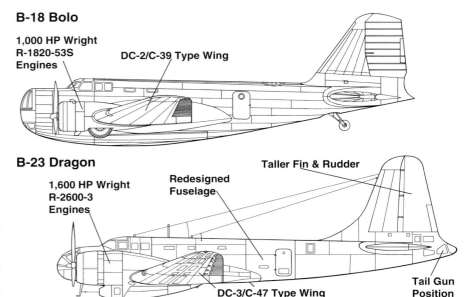

1,000 HP Wright R-1820-53S Engines

DC-2/C-39 Type Wing

B-23 Dragon

Taller Fin & Rudder

1,600 HP Wright R-2600-3 Engines

Redesigned Fuselage

DC-3/C-47 Type Wing

Tail Gun Position

first unit equipped with the B-23. One bomb group was completely operational with the B-23 Dragon, the 17th Bombardment Group at McChord Field, Washington. But the service career of the B-23 was short-lived as the 17th BG soon replaced their B-23s with North American B-25 Mitchell bombers during late 1941. Conversion to the B-25 by the 17th BG crews was completed just in time for their participation in the famous Doolittle Raid on Japan in April of 1942. At least eighteen of the obsolete B-18s had all their offensive and defensive armament systems removed and were modified for use as staff and VIP transport aircraft, with the designation of UC-67. Several B-23s were used to conduct glider pickup tests. These B-23s were fitted with a long hook to snag the glider pickup cable that was stretched between two poles on the ground. These tests were later used operationally by both Army Air Force C-47 and Royal Air Force Dakota units.

A Douglas B-23 on the Clover Field ramp after the beginning of the war. Although much faster than the B-18, the B-23 was still not competitive with bombers like the North American B-25 and Martin B-26. The B-23s were relegated to test and/or training missions. (Leo Kohn)

DC-3/C-47 Variants

The Douglas DC-3 was a direct result of the fierce airline competition in the mid-1930s. TWA had the DC-2, the finest passenger airplane in the world, American Airlines did not and neither did United Airlines. Additionally. they really didn't want the exact same aircraft as TWA. American Airlines wanted a flying version of the Pullman Railway Car, a sleeper airplane and the DC-2 could not meet their requirements. Specifically American Airlines wanted an airplane with a much greater passenger capacity than the DC-2, with the cabin area capable of conversion to sleeper berths, and an airplane with both greater range and better stability than the DC-2 offered.

Douglas answered the American Airlines requirements with the Douglas Sleeper Transport, or DST. The DST was twenty-six inches wider than the DC-2 through the cabin area. Most of this was accomplished by simply "rounding" the fuselage sides. Additionally, the fuselage was lengthened some two and a half feet. The wings were strengthened and the span was increased by a full ten feet. The new wings had tapered, rounded tips, much longer ailerons, and increased internal fuel tankage, thus increasing the range. The directional control problems that had surfaced during the development of the DC-2 were solved by increasing the area of the vertical tail and rudder assembly. The horizontal stabilizer and elevator assembly were likewise increased in area. The DST was powered by a pair of Wright SGR-1820-G engines rated at 850 horsepower, with 1,000 horsepower available for takeoff. The DST made its first flight on 17 December 1935.

Several civilian airliner variants were based on the DST design, each one varying according to seating capacity and style, and engine types. The DST could hold up to twenty-eight passengers for a daylight flight, or fourteen for a night flight using the convertible seats as berths. The DST-A was virtually identical except that it was powered by Pratt and Whitney SB-G (R-1830) Twin Wasp engines rated at 1,000 horsepower. The pure daylight transport aircraft were the first to carry the designation of DC-3. They differed from the DST in having non-convertible passenger seats accommodating up to twenty-eight passengers. The DC-3s were powered by Wright SGR-1820 Cyclone engines rated at 1,000 horsepower. The DC-3A was an identical aircraft, but powered by Pratt and Whitney SIC-S Twin Wasp engines rated at 1,000 horsepower. Finally there was the DC-3B, which had half convertible seating, and half standard passenger seats. The DC-3Bs had Wright Cyclone power.

C-41A

All military versions were based on one of the civilian passenger aircraft types, no matter what the military designation was. And the first in the series was not a C-47, it was the Douglas C-41A. The C-41A was a standard DC-3A with Pratt and Whitney R-1830-21 engines, a military version of the SC-G Twin Wasp, rated at 1,200 horsepower in War Emergency setting. It differed from its civilian counterparts in having military equipment like instrumentation and radios, and had swivel seating in the passenger cabin. Only one C-41A was built, being delivered to the Army Air Corps in September of 1939. Following complete testing at Wright Field, the C-41A was delivered to Headquarters, 1st Staff Squadron at Bolling Field, just outside of Washington, DC, where it was used as a staff and VIP transport.

The first American Airlines Douglas DST (Douglas Sleeper Transport) on the ramp at Floyd Bennett Field, New York during 1936. The DST was longer and wider than the DC-2, with the "round" fuselage sides. This aircraft was the first of what is universally considered the DC-3 series. (Vincent Berinati)

C-47

The C-47-DL was the military version of the DST/DC-3 airliner aircraft. The C-47-DL was actually developed from the DST-A/DC-3A type as it was powered by Pratt and Whitney military engines, the 1,200 horsepower (in War Emergency) R-1830-92 Twin Wasp engine. Externally the C-47-DL differed mainly in having the small passenger entry door replaced by a large, three section cargo door on the port side of the fuselage to the rear of the wing trailing

Fuselage Development

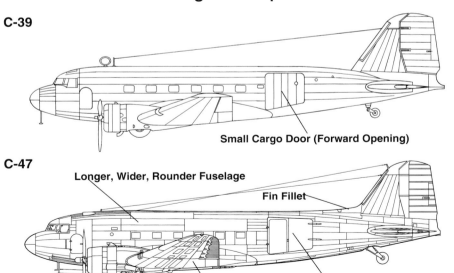

C-39

Small Cargo Door (Forward Opening)

C-47

Longer, Wider, Rounder Fuselage

Fin Fillet

Longer, Tapered Wing   Larger Split Cargo Door

edge. The forward door section could be opened entirely, or a smaller entry door within the larger door could be used, similar to a airliner door. Many times the entire forward door was completely removed during operations. Along with the larger cargo door, a C-47-DL had a six inch greater wingspan and an astrodome on the upper fuselage just behind the cockpit.

Internally all the plushness was gone. The comfortable airliner seating was replaced with twenty-eight small canvas seats that folded up against the fuselage wall. These canvas seats gave way to metal seats later in the long operational career of the C-47. For heavy cargo hauling, the main floor in the cabin area was reinforced and had tie down rings at certain points to hold cargo in place. Some had cargo hooks added to the underside of the wing center section that could hold large, bulky cargo items. Internally, a C-47-DL could be outfitted as a flying ambulance, with a capacity of up to fourteen litter patients. Up to 6,000 pounds of cargo could be handled, which might include a complete Jeep and trailer or 37MM anti-tank gun.

The first C-47-DL was delivered to Army Air Force sixteen days after Pearl Harbor. It was the first of nine hundred and sixty-five C-47-DL aircraft. But these were only the first of a total of over 10,000 aircraft based on the initial design. The Navy/Marine equivalent to the C-

The first military transport based on the DST/DC-3 was the C-41A, which was delivered to the Army Air Corps in September of 1939. The C-41A was actually based on a DC-3A with Pratt & Whitney R-1830 Twin Wasp radial engines. (AFM)

The C-47 Skytrain was the production version of the military DC-3A, having a three-section cargo door on the rear fuselage. Most C-47s had folding canvas or metal seats to accommodate up to twenty-eight fully equipped combat troops. The aircraft has an astrodome and air intake scoop on the upper fuselage behind the cockpit and dust filters on the upper engine cowlings. (Don Garrett Jr)

Although labeled a C-47-DL, this Skytrain has a passenger airliner rear entry door, indicating that it was an "impressed" DC-3A in Army service in North Africa during 1942. Many airliners were "drafted" into war service when Douglas production could not keep up with the demand. (Norm Taylor)

The interior of a C-47 with folding metal seats. Originally, the comfortable airliner seating was replaced with twenty-eight small canvas seats that folded up against the fuselage wall. These canvas seats gave way to metal seats later in the long operational career of the C-47. (AFM)

The front instrument panel of a production C-47 showing the typical Douglas automobile type control wheel and center console with engine and propeller controls. (AFM)

A C-47-DL of the 433rd Troop Carrier Group sits next to a destroyed Ki-43 Oscar fighter at Hollandia Airstrip during April 1944. The C-47 could carry up to 6,000 pounds of cargo. (James F. Lansdale)

This pair of C-47-DLs were assigned to the 306th TCS/442 TCG based at Fulbeck, England during 1944. Both aircraft have additional parachute cargo "bundles" attached under the wing center section. (James V. Crow)

27

A RAF Dakota of No 267 Squadron takes on passengers at an Egyptian airdrome during 1944. The aircraft carries a Desert Air Force camouflage scheme of Dark Earth and Middlestone uppersurfaces over Azure Blue undersurfaces with Red squadron codes. (James V. Crow)

Shanghai Lil prepares for takeoff from Ward's Drome airfield near Port Moresby, New Guinea during April of 1943 after unloading badly needed supplies for the troops at Wau. *Lil* was a C-47-DL from the 6th TCS/374th TCG. (USAF)

47-DL was the R4D-1. These were virtually identical to the Army aircraft, except for having Navy-specified instrumentation and radios. They were also powered by Pratt and Whitney Twin Wasp engines rated at 1,200 horsepower. The first R4D-1 was delivered in February of 1942. Only the initial sixty six R4D-1s came on a Navy-ordered contract. The next forty

A pair of R4D-1s of the Marine Corps South Pacific Air Transport (SCAT) force enroute to Green Island from Bouganville in March of 1943. Navy/Marine R4D-1s were virtually identical to Army C-47-DLs, even having Army Olive Drab and Neutral Gray camouflage. (USMC)

R4D-1s came on an Army contract and were then transferred to the Navy.

The C-47A differed from both the C-47-DL and R4D-1 in having a 24 volt electrical system and improved cabin heating. More C-47As were built than any other variant, with a total of 5,253 being built at the two Douglas factories. The C-47B was a high altitude variant for use in the China/Burma/India Theater, flying the "Hump" route. They had two stage superchargers added to the Twin Wasp engines, now designated R-1830-90C, Douglas built 3,252 C-47Bs by the end of the war. There was no Navy equivalent to the C-47A or C-47B. The C-47D was simply a C-47B that had the high blower portion of the two stage supercharger removed; i.e., the C-47Ds were conversions of existing C-47B airframes.

A RAF Dakota ready to "snatch" a USAAF CG-4A Waco glider into the air during glider pickup demonstrations prior to D-Day. The hook on the Dakota would snag the tow cable of the glider, which was stretched between two upright poles. (AFM)

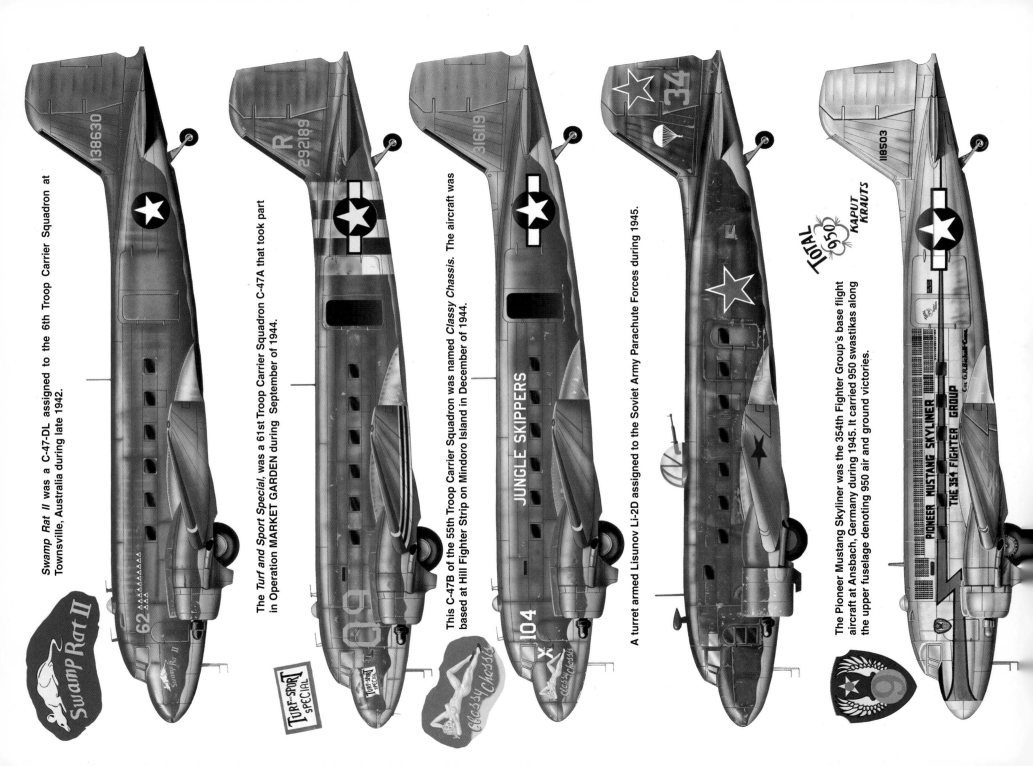

Swamp Rat II was a C-47-DL assigned to the 6th Troop Carrier Squadron at Townsville, Australia during late 1942.

The *Turf and Sport Special*, was a 61st Troop Carrier Squadron C-47A that took part in Operation MARKET GARDEN during September of 1944.

This C-47B of the 55th Troop Carrier Squadron was named *Classy Chassis*. The aircraft was based at Hill Fighter Strip on Mindoro Island in December of 1944.

A turret armed Lisunov Li-2D assigned to the Soviet Army Parachute Forces during 1945.

The Pioneer Mustang Skyliner was the 354th Fighter Group's base flight aircraft at Ansbach, Germany during 1945. It carried 950 swastikas along the upper fuselage denoting 950 air and ground victories.

A Dakota Mk I of No 267 Pegasus Squadron, Desert Air Force . The unit was based in Egypt during 1942.

Anything, Anywhere, Anytime, was a C-47A Dakota of No 40 Transport Squadron, Royal New Zealand Air Force at Auckland, NZ during 1944.

This early FC-47 was named 'Git-em' Bullett and was assigned to the 4th Air Commando Squaron at Bien Hoa during late 1965. The aircraft was armed with ten .30 caliber machine guns.

I Must Go was one of the highly classified EC-47N electronic warfare aircraft of the 360th TEWS at Phu Cat, South Vietnam during 1970.

The Kool Kiwi was one of the U. S. Navy's Antarctica explorer LC-47Ms assigned to VX-6 at Christ Church, New Zealand during 1967.

"Wing Tip Willie", was a C-47A of the 96th TCS/440th TCG based at Exeter, England in the Summer of 1944. The C-47A differed from earlier variants in that it was equipped with a 24 volt electfical system. (USAF)

C-48, C-49, C-50, C-53, C-117

Wing Development

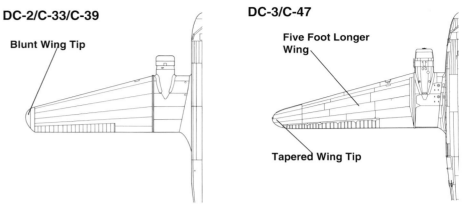

DC-2/C-33/C-39

Blunt Wing Tip

DC-3/C-47

Five Foot Longer Wing

Tapered Wing Tip

This is where the story gets more than a little muddy. At the beginning of the war both Army and Navy wanted the new Douglas transports immediately, meaning yesterday! Douglas was building them as fast as possible, but simply could not meet the growing demand. Many civilian airliners were still on the Douglas assembly line, having been on order prior to the Pearl Harbor attack. With a simple stroke of the pen, the War Department "impressed" all these DST/DC-3 civilian airliners into military service. They were, in effect, drafted and given military designations. Eleven aircraft originally built for United, Pan Am, and others, were "impressed" and designated C-48. These were all Twin Wasp powered DC-3As with various seating arrangements. An additional twenty-five DC-3As already in service with various airlines, were also "impressed" into service as C-48s.

The C-49 designation went to all the Wright Cyclone powered airliners that were "impressed" into service. Seventy-five aircraft on the Douglas assembly line were "impressed" as C-49s. Two Eastern Airlines DC-3s were "impressed" as staff transports for the Navy, with the designation R4D-2. An additional sixty-three in-service DC-3s also became C-49s. The fourteen C-50s were all taken from the assembly line. These were all Wright Cyclone powered DC-3s. The sole C-51 was a Can Col DC-3. Five DC-3As originally intended for service with Eastern, Western, and United Airlines were "impressed" as C-52s. The sixth C-52 was an in-service draftee. There were two different C-53 aircraft types. Seventeen airline DC-3As were "impressed" as C-53Cs, with a further ten being "impressed" into Navy service as R4D-4.

The initial C-53 designation went to a purpose-built troop transport aircraft. The C-53 Skytrooper did not have the large triple-opening cargo door as seen on the C-47 cargo types. The C-53 had a small passenger-type entry door on the port fuselage. The C-53 had twenty-eight small metal bucket seats laid out airliner-style in the cabin. The floor was not reinforced, as on the cargo hauling C-47 types since the C-53 was built to move troops. Some aircraft had the small tail fairing removed and were fitted with a reinforced cleat for use as a glider tug. The C-53s were powered by Pratt and Whitney R-1830-92 engines rated at 1,200 horsepower. Douglas built two hundred twenty-one C-53s, twenty of which were transferred to the Navy as R4D-3s. There were eight aircraft built as C-53Bs. These were a winterized version slated for operations in the Alaskan Theater. Besides the winterizing equipment, the

C-53Bs had additional fuel tanks and an astrodome for the navigator, which had been omitted from normal production C-53s. The C-53D had the small metal seats attached to the fuselage wall. Douglas built one hundred fifty-nine C-53Ds. Two DC-3As were "impressed" as C-68s. And an additional twelve aircraft from Pan American Airways were "impressed" but given no designation. The C-84 was a designation given to four "impressed" in-service DC-3s.

A requirement for a more plush transport type for Army use brought about the initial C-117 designation. The C-117 was a combination of C-47B and C-53 types, in that they were powered by Pratt and Whitney R-1830-90C engines with the two stage supercharger for high altitude operations, but had only the small passenger-style entry door found on the C-53. Internally the C-117 did not have the reinforced flooring of a cargo aircraft, and were fitted with the more comfortable airliner-type seats. Some were outfitted with swivel seating for high level staff meetings in-flight. The C-117B was the same aircraft with the upper stage of the supercharger removed.

Several VC-47A staff transports were overhauled and brought to C-117B standards. Finally came the C-117D, a military version of the Douglas Super DC-3.

RAF Dakota Mk IIIs from No. 267 Pegasus Squadron line the ramp at a base in Italy in 1944. The Dakota Mk III was the RAF equivilant to the C-47A. Other aircraft on the field include USAAF P-47s, P-38s, P-51s, B-24s and a single B-17. (IWM)

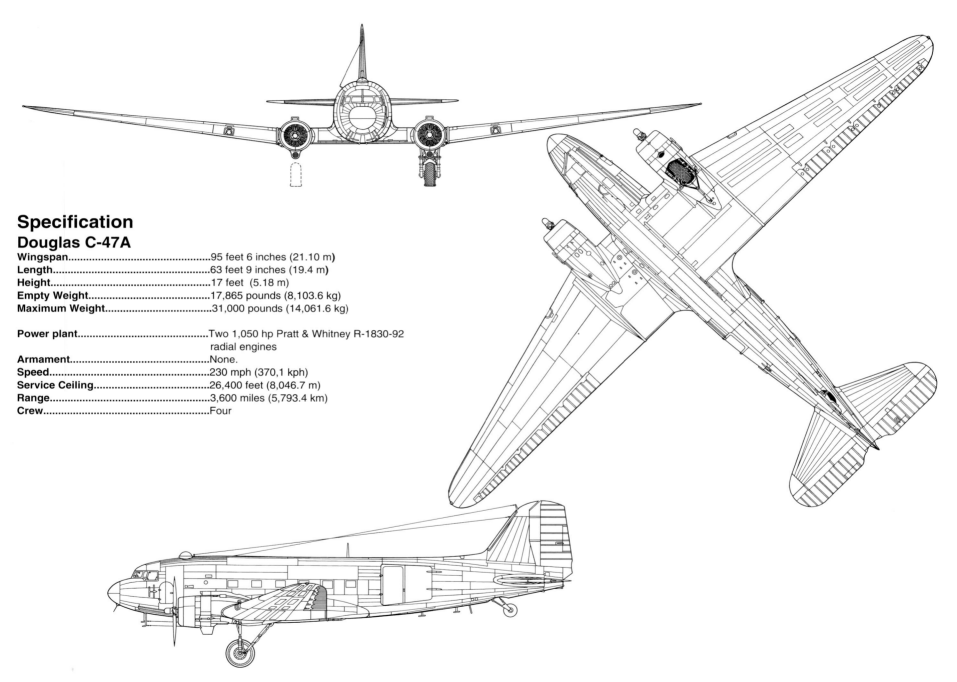

Specification
Douglas C-47A
Wingspan..95 feet 6 inches (21.10 m**)**
Length...63 feet 9 inches (19.4 m**)**
Height...17 feet (5.18 m)
Empty Weight..17,865 pounds (8,103.6 kg)
Maximum Weight.....................................31,000 pounds (14,061.6 kg)

Power plant..Two 1,050 hp Pratt & Whitney R-1830-92
                                                                              radial engines
Armament..None.
Speed..230 mph (370,1 kph)
Service Ceiling..26,400 feet (8,046.7 m)
Range..3,600 miles (5,793.4 km)
Crew...Four

A C-47A from the China Air Task Force on the ramp at Hsein, China during 1945. The CATF was a joint U.S./China composite force. The aircraft is equipped with additional antennas and a directional loop antenna common to CBI Theater aircraft. (George McKay)

Australian troops load a jeep into the cargo hold of a Royal Australian Air Force (RAAF) Dakota Mk III in Southeast Asia Command markings. The C-47 could carry a jeep and trailer or a Jeep and 37mm anti-tank gun. (IWM)

The *"Chastity Chariot"* was a RAF Dakota based at Imphal, India during 1943. The British government obtained a total of some 1,928 Dakota Mk IIIs during the war. (AFM)

Lady Veta and other C-47As from the 305th TCS/442nd TCG line the ramp at Weston Zoyland RAF base on 5 June 1944. The distinctive Black and White stripes were hastily added to all tactical aircraft immediately prior to D-Day. (James V. Crow)

Even the "old lady" got tired and had to be retired. This C-47A from the 305th TCS, veteran of five 82nd Airborne Division drops and numerous re-supply missions, sits forlornly in the junkyard at Munchen-Reim amid the remains of Hitler's' vaunted Luftwaffe. (James V. Crow)

Members of the 101st Airborne Division prepare to board a C-47A from the 98th TCS/440th TCG at Exeter, England, in the early evening of 5 June 1944. Hours later the men of both the 82nd and 101st Airborne Divisions would be the first Allied troops to land in Europe. (AFM)

A RCAF Dakota Mk III from No 435 Squadron, Combat Cargo Task Force, carries supplies both internally and on the underwing racks for the British and Chindit forces fighting the Japanese in Burma. (IWM)

Cowling & Dust Filter Development

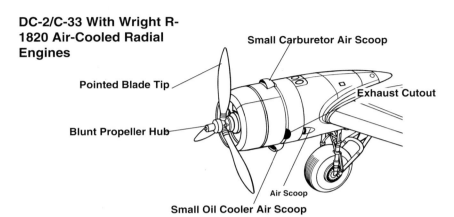

DC-2/C-33 With Wright R-1820 Air-Cooled Radial Engines

Small Carburetor Air Scoop

Pointed Blade Tip

Exhaust Cutout

Blunt Propeller Hub

Air Scoop

Small Oil Cooler Air Scoop

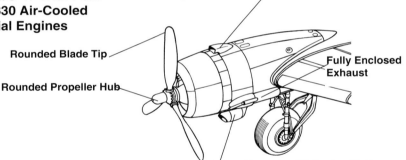

DC-3/C-47 With P&W R-1830 Air-Cooled Radial Engines

Larger Carburetor Air Scoop

Rounded Blade Tip

Fully Enclosed Exhaust

Rounded Propeller Hub

Larger/Rounder Oil Cooler Air Scoop

C-47 With P&W R-1830   **C-47 With P&W R-1830**

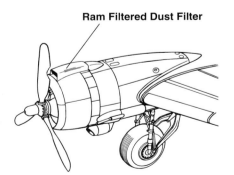

Ram Filtered Dust Filter

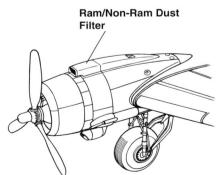

Ram/Non-Ram Dust Filter

The *Turf Sport Special* was a C-47A of the 61st TCS/314th TCG over Holland during Operation MARKET GARDEN in September of 1944. The upper surface D-Day stripes were overpainted with Olive Drab, which rapidly faded. (Jeff Ethell)

Several C-47As were equipped with a Bombing Through Overcast (BTO) radar, acting as Lead Ships for the D-Day and Market Garden operations. This C-47A "Lead" flying over Holland 8 September 1944, is from the 36th TCS/316th TCG. (Ed Howe)

Hard Ships, a C-47A from the 35th Fighter Group on the ramp at Kim-Po Air Base, near Seoul, Korea during 1945. Five years later Kimpo would be filled with not only C-47s, but all types of United Nation aircraft attempting to stop a new world aggressor, North Korea. (Art Krieger)

A D-Day veteran C-47A assigned to the North Atlantic Wing, Military Air Transport Command unloads cargo in the Panama Canal Zone during 1945. Douglas built more C-47As than any other variant, with a total of 5,233 coming off the two Douglas assembly lines. (Warren Bodie)

(Left) A trio of 433rd Troop Carrier Group C-47As fly over the ocean near the seaplane ramp at Hollandia in early 1944. X153 in the background retains the Red outlined national insignia first authorized during 1943. (John Stanaway)

These C-47Bs were assigned to the 317th Troop Carrier Squadron (Commando) at Hailakaudi, India during 1944. The engines on the C-47B had two stage superchargers to give them the additional power that was needed to fly the Hump routes. (Jeff Ethell)

S for Sugar, a Dakota Mk III from No 267 Pegasus Squadron flies over the Grecian islands near Yugoslavia during January of 1945. RAF Dakotas dropped supplies to Balkan troops fighting the Germans under the auspices of the Balkan Air Force. (IWM)

A U. S. Marine SCAT R4D-3, the equivalent to the Army C-53, lifts off from Espirito Santo during 1944. Navy/Marine R4Ds were usually painted in Army Olive Drab and Neutral Gray, although there were several that carried the Navy three-tone Blue camouflage. (Jim Sullivan)

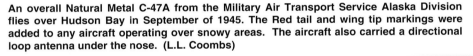

A 90th TCS/438th TCG C-47 yanks a Horsa glider into the air at RAF Greenham Common during the early hours of 6 June 1944. Many C-47s had the tail cone removed and were fitted with a reinforced glider-towing hook. (Jeff Ethell)

An overall Natural Metal C-47A from the Military Air Transport Service Alaska Division flies over Hudson Bay in September of 1945. The Red tail and wing tip markings were added to any aircraft operating over snowy areas. The aircraft also carried a directional loop antenna under the nose. (L.L. Coombs)

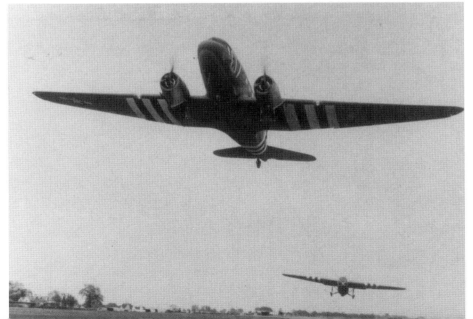

A C-48 of the 1st Staff Squadron at Bolling Field, outside Washington, DC during 1942. C-48s were all "impressed" DC-3As from various airlines used as VIP transports. The aircraft in the background is a United Air Lines Boeing 247. (Art Krieger)

An "impressed" DC-3, Army designation C-49, from the SEACTC at Bolling Field, during 1942. The aircraft carried standard Army camouflage of Olive Drab over Neutral Gray. The War Department "impressed" 140 DC-3/DC-3As as C-49/R4D-2s during the war. (Jack Binder)

(Left) This C-53-DO on the ramp at Lubbock Field, Texas in 1943, carries the markings of a trainer aircraft with Yellow bands on the nose, wing tips and fuselage. The C-53-DO was an "impressed" DC-3A without airliner seats. (Norm Taylor via Nick Williams)

An overall Natural Metal C-117A-DK at a stateside field during mid-1945. The C-117A was a slightly more plush military transport developed for the Army. The aircraft had an airliner passenger entry door in place of the large cargo doors common to C-47s. (Leo Kohn)

This C-47A was flown by members of the Free French Air Forces supporting French Army ground operations in the war. The aircraft carries French roundels and tri-color fin flash on the tail, but otherwise was painted in standard USAAF colors. (James V. Crow)

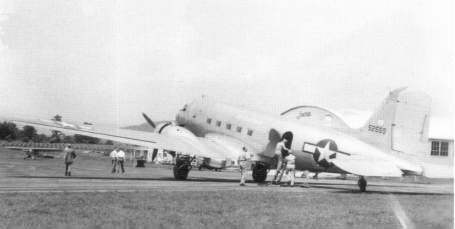

C-47, 433rd Troop Carrier Group, Hollandia 1944. (John Stanaway)

C-47, Headquarters Squadron, 50th TCG, France, 1944. (James V. Crow)

C-47, 441st TCG, 9th AF, France, 1944. (James V. Crow)

C-47, 809th TCS, England, 1944. (James V. Crow)

Nose Art:

Nose act was abundant on C-47 aircraft in all theaters of war during the Second World War. It was found on USAAF, USN, Marine Corps as well as British transports. Nose art could be anything from the comical to the profane; however, the female form was perhaps the most popular form of nose art.

C-47, 81st TCS, France, 1944. (AFM)

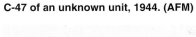

C-47 of an unknown unit, 1944. (AFM)

C-47, unknown unit, Saipan, 1945. (James V. Crow)

C-47, 367th TCG, 1944. (AFM)

39

The XC-47C had the normal wheeled landing gear replaced with EDO Corporation floats. The EDO Corporation made some 150 sets of floats and a number of C-47Cs were operational in both the South Pacific and Alaska Theaters. (Nick Williams)

Five years after the end of the Second World War, the venerable Gooney Birds were again in combat in a small desolate country named Korea. This 21st TCS C-47B was delivering supplies to the U.S. 24th Infantry Division after the recapture of Taejon in late September of 1950. (USAF)

The XCG-17 glider was a C-47-DL with the engines removed and faired over. Planned as a combat glider capable of holding up to 15,000 pounds of cargo, the XCG-17 never went beyond the prototype stage. As such; however, it was the biggest and best performing glider of the war. (AFM)

Marine Corps R4Ds were also operational in the Korean War. This R4D-5 was assigned to the 1st Marine Air Wing in 1953. Marine R4Ds hauled supplies and troops and were also used as night flareships over the front lines. (USMC)

C-47s were readily available to any NATO air force during the rebuilding years after the end of the Second World War. This Danish Air Force C-47 was painted Olive Green (RAL 6014) and Basalt Gray (RAL 7012) with Light Gray undersurfaces. (William Peters)

The KOOL KIWI was a LC-47H assigned to VX-6 at Christchurch, New Zealand in December of 1967. The enlarged radome housed a search radar to locate and track incoming missiles and payloads for NASA. (Jim Sullivan)

This C-47D was assigned as a base flight aircraft with the 509th Bomb Wing, SAC during 1968. The C-47D was a C-47B with a modified supercharger. The aircraft has had rotating beacons added to the top of the tail and under the fuselage. (Frank MacSorley)

C-47s were supplied to the Israeli Defense Force/Air Force (IDF/AF) during the late 1950s as their primary cargo mover. The camouflage was Tan (FS 30219), Light Green (FS 34227), and Yellow (FS 33531). (Don Garrett Jr.)

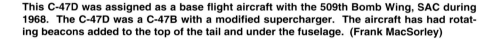

41

A United Nations Dakota from the Royal Canadian Air Force. C-47s and Dakotas were used by UN relief forces to bring supplies to starving nations such as Biafra. The UN Dakotas were painted overall White with Medium Blue lettering and UN logos. (Terry Love)

It's hard to believe that the U.S. was ever friendly enough with the Libyan government to supply them with C-47 aircraft through the Military Assistance Plan. This Libyan C-47 was painted Silver, with a White top and Black lettering. (William Peters)

An attempt to add still more life to the ageing RAF Dakota fleet came in the form of adding Rolls Royce Mamba turboprop engines in longer, streamlined cowlings. Efforts to re-engine the C-47 with turboprops still go on today. (Robert Esposito)

A C-47D with the West German Bundesluftwaffe during 1970. The WGAF had both C-47s and Dakotas in their inventory. This example was painted Silver and White, with a Dark Blue cheat !ine and Day glo Orange bands on the fuselage, wing tips, and rudder. (Don Garrett Jr.)

Pinocchio was one of several Royal Canadian Air Force Dakotas modified with the nose and radar from a Bomarc surface-to-air missile system. They were used as both test and trainer aircraft for RCAF Bomarc crews. (Philip Tachauer)

One of several C-47s that the Argentine Air Force used during their exploration of Antarctica in the 1960s. The Argentine C-47 had skis mounted on all wheels, and had the nose, tail, and wing tips painted Red for high visibility in the snow covered country. (Leo Kohn)

A Navy R4D-6Q electronic warfare aircraft on the ramp at Nha Trang during mid-1964. The pug-nose radome housed a radar receiver used to locate and monitor North Vietnamese radio/radar emissions. The aircraft had additional windows behind the cockpit and in the forward crew entry door. (Al Adcock)

43

A highly polished Douglas Dakota of F8 Squadron, Swedish Air Force, on the ramp at Uppsale, Sweden during June of 1968. The aircraft has an additional astrodome and many different antennas. The nose, fuselage bands, and wing tips are Gloss International Orange. (Don Garrett)

A beautiful C-47 assigned to NASA and carrying the Medium Blue outlined in Red cheat line dividing the Gloss White top from the Gloss Gray (FS 16440) bottom. NASA C-47s had varied missions, from hauling space 'junk' to astronauts. (Jim Sullivan)

Mexicano was a highly modified C-47A assigned to the Mexican Air Force Presidential Flight. The C-47 has clipped wing tips, a large single entry door, and short exhaust stacks. The colors were Green and White, with Red trim. (Don Garrett)

A Nicaraguan Air Force C-47D on the ramp at Davis-Monthan Air Force Base during July of 1975. C-47s were rushed to the Samozan government during the Nicaraguan civil war of the mid-1970s to aid the government in its fight with the Sandanistas. (Tom Brewer Collection)

A Cambodian Air Force C-47B on the Tan Son Nhut ramp during December of 1970. The Cambodian Air Force used trash hauler, gunship, and "electric goons", all of which were ex-USAF Vietnam veterans. (Norm Taylor)

A C-47D assigned to the U.S. Army Missile Command on the ramp at Orlando, Florida in February of 1972. The Army had very few C-47 aircraft compared with their fleet during the Second World War, since most of the fixed-wing aircraft were assigned to the Air Force and Navy/Marines by law. The colors are Gloss Olive Drab and White, with Black trim. (William Strandberg)

The largest airline operation in Southeast Asia by far was Air America. Air America C-47s hauled supplies, dropped agents, flew search and rescue missions, and were used as airborne command posts over ground units in contact with whatever enemy was at hand. The aircraft carried the term 'CHARTERED' on the fuselage under the America logo. (Lieutenant Colonel Barry Miller)

45

Foreign-built Variants

Several foreign manufacturers acquired the manufacturing and distributions rights for the Douglas Commercial and military transport aircraft, including the Germans, Russians and Japanese. The biggest non-U.S. user of the Douglas transport was the United Kingdom. Those aircraft, used by RAF, RAAF, and RCAF, were all direct purchases from Douglas Aircraft Company. The British variants were known as Dakotas, and all were based on USAAF C-47 types, with the exception being the forty-five DC-2/C-89 aircraft that the RAF and RAAF acquired from U.S. airline inventories at the beginning of the war. None of the DC-2/C-89 aircraft were designated as Dakotas. The British government acquired 1,928 Dakota-type aircraft throughout the war. The Dakota Mk I was equivalent to the C-47-DL, Dakota Mk II being a copy of the C-53-DO, the Dakota III was a C-47A-DL or -DK, and the Dakota Mk IV was based on the C-47B-DK. Any civilian DC-3 airliners "impressed" into British military service were also designated as Dakotas.

Of the foreign manufacturers that actually built the Douglas transport under license, Fokker had the European rights and Mitsui & Co. the Far East rights. Fokker built thirty-nine DC-2 aircraft that were used by KLM, Swissair, and Lufthansa. Fokker also acquired the rights to build the DC-3, but none were ever actually built. Several DC-3s; however, were maintained by Fokker personnel both before and during the war.

The Mitsui and Co. Ltd held the Japanese rights to build the DC-3, while Nakajima had the DC-2 rights. Twenty Douglas-built DC-3s/DC-3As were disassembled and shipped to Japan for use as pattern aircraft. Mitsui and Co. Ltd then had the Showa Aircraft Co. re-assemble the aircraft and set up an assembly line. Showa built a total of 414 military transports, designated the L2D, for the Imperial Japanese Navy. Code-named Tabby by the Allies, the L2D differed from a Douglas-built aircraft in being powered by Mitsubishi Kinsei engines, a copy of the Pratt & Whitney R-1830 Twin Wasp. Many of the production aircraft had additional windows behind the cockpit, propeller spinners, a smaller cargo door, and some had a dorsal blister mounting a single 13MM machine gun. The Kinsei engines had slightly different engine cowlings, with large exhaust pipes exiting just aft of the cowl flaps. Though Showa was the primary Japanese manufacturer, it was Nakajima that built the first seventy-one Tabbys when the Showa production line was slow in opening.

The Lisunov type 2, or Li-2, was the license-built variant for use by air forces of the Soviet Union during the war. The Li-2 was powered by a pair of Shvetsov M-62 or ASh-62 engines, license copies of the Wright R-1820 Cyclone. Originally designated the PS-84, the Lisunov company built 2,930 Li-2s during the war. The external differences between a U.S. C-47 and a Lisunov Li-2 were similar to those found on the Japanese Tabby. The engine cowlings resembled those of a Wright Cyclone-powered DC-3, with different shaped scoops for both the carburetor and the oil cooler. The cargo doors were moved forward one full fuselage station and were of a different shape. Passenger versions of the Li-2 had the entry door on the starboard side, rather than on the port side as on U.S. C-47s, and many had additional windows behind the cockpit in various configurations.

The Li-2 was the first to have a permanent defensive armament capability. Both U.S. and Japanese types had portable machine gun mounts that allowed troops to fire through the cabin windows. But the Li-2 had a large manual turret on top of the fuselage mounting either a single 12.7MM (.50 caliber) or 7.62MM (.30 caliber) machine gun. Some had an additional window in the rear fuselage on both sides of the fuselage mounting a single machine gun. This reasonably heavily armed Li-2 was used as a night bomber aircraft in addition to being a troop transport. In this role, the Li-2 had external bomb racks under the wing center section that could hold up to 4,000 pounds of bombs. Additionally, many had underwing rocket launchers added to the outer wing panels. Even when flown in the bomber role, the Li-2 was still capa-

Fuselage Development

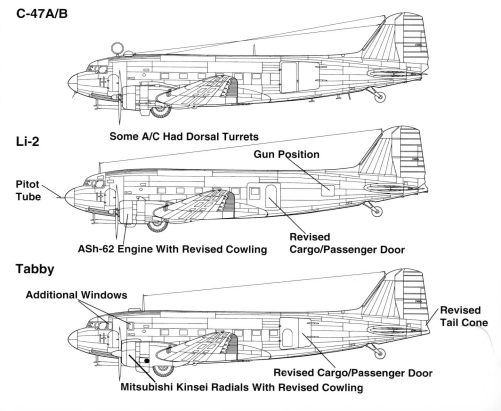

C-47A/B

Some A/C Had Dorsal Turrets

Li-2

Gun Position

Pitot Tube

ASh-62 Engine With Revised Cowling

Revised Cargo/Passenger Door

Tabby

Additional Windows

Revised Tail Cone

Mitsubishi Kinsei Radials With Revised Cowling

Revised Cargo/Passenger Door

The Soviet Union obtained many Douglas-built C-47s under Lend-Lease during the Second World War. This Lend-Lease C-47 carried Soviet diplomats on its return flight to the U.S. during 1946. (Hans-Heiri Stapfer)

Russian civilian passengers about to board a Soviet Li-2 passenger aircraft. The passenger version of the Li-2 was virtually identical to a Wright-powered DC-3. The camouflage colors are Dark Green and Dark Brown. (Hans-Heiri Stapfer)

ble of transporting up to twenty Soviet troops. The standard transport variant could hold up to twenty-five fully equipped troops. Performance was less than a standard C-47, mostly due to the additional weight of the defensive armament and overall heavier weight of the Li-2s construction. The Li-2 saw service throughout the war on all fronts and served both Soviet and Eastern Bloc countries as a troop transport well into the 1980s.

(Right) A Nakajima-built L2D Tess on the ramp at the Tokyo Airport in the early 1945. The Nakajima L2D was a license copy of the DC-2. This Tess was camouflaged in Green and Brown, with a White fuselage band and Hinomarus on the wings. (Haru Kurusan)

Lisunov-built Li-2s were often armed with a manually operated 12.7MM upper gun turret, along with a pair of 7.62MM waist guns mounted in the windows at the rear of the fuselage.

Engine Cowling

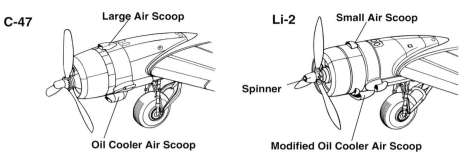

C-47 — Large Air Scoop, Oil Cooler Air Scoop

Li-2 — Small Air Scoop, Spinner, Modified Oil Cooler Air Scoop

A Yugoslavian Air Force Li-2 on the ramp at Munchen-Peim, Germany during the Summer of 1945. The Li-2 was powered by a pair of Shvetsov ASh-62 engines, a licensed copy of the Wright Cyclone. (James V. Crow)

The Showa-built L2D type 0 was a copy of the DC-3A, powered by Mitsubishi Kinsel engines, a license copy of the Pratt & Whitney Twin Wasp. Code-named Tabby, the L2Ds had additional windows behind the cockpit. (DOD)

Special Operations Aircraft

The C-47 has been flown in virtually every conceivable mission the military can dream up — from transport to fighter to electronic warfare to Psywar. This section will cover those types that were either designed from the outset for a specific mission, or were converted for a new mission in substantial numbers.

SC-47

The SC-47 was a standard C-47 transport configured for the search and rescue mission. The aircraft carried inflatable life rafts, which were thrown to victims from the open rear cargo hatch. The rafts were inflated after leaving the aircraft. The SC-47s also carried flares, additional food and water, waterproof radios, and other essential rescue equipment. Some SC-47s had para-rescue crew members (PJs) who would parachute over a downed pilot and assist him with his rescue. The pilot and PJ were then picked up by either a helicopter or amphibious aircraft, like the Grumman SA-16 Albatros. SC-47s operating from Alaska or other very cold climates could be fitted with skis for snow operations. SC-47s were very active during the Korean War, operating from places like Cho-Do Island off the coast of North Korea, some fifty miles north of the main battle lines. The SC-47 was later redesignated the HC-47.

AC-47

There were two separate, and very distinctively different aircraft with the designation of AC-47. One type listened intently, while the other talked with a load voice, a very load voice. The first twenty-six C-47Ds were converted to AC-47Ds by the Hayes Corporation during 1953. They were used by the Air Force Airways and Communications Service, or AACS. These aircraft were crammed with electronic monitoring equipment including an IFF radar identification system, a weather avoidance radar in the nose, radio compass, LORAN, TACAN, radio direction finder, marker beacon, and a multitude of radios on both the UHF and VHF channels. The mission of the AC-47 was to monitor radio and radar frequencies originating from Soviet sources behind the Iron Curtain. During 1962, the AC-47 became first the RC-47D (R for reconnaissance), then the EC-47D (E for Electronic).

The war in Vietnam saw several more electronic variants of the C-47, which were commonly referred to as "Electric Goons." The EC-47N differed greatly from the earlier AC/RC/EC-47D. Externally, the long radar nose was changed to a shorter radome, and the aircraft was covered with wire antenna leads. No less than six antenna wires ran from both sides of the vertical tail to antenna stubs around the upper forward fuselage on some aircraft. There were whip antennas for System X above and below the cockpit, and above and below each wing outboard of the engine nacelles. The fuselage had FM Command Net whip aerials on top of the fuselage and UHF, TACAN, VHF, and IFF blade antennas were mounted above and below the fuselage. Internally, there were four electronic warfare consoles, one each for System X, System Y, System Z-1/Q-1 and System Z-2/Q-2. Each system monitored a different and highly classified portion of the North Vietnamese/Viet Cong radio or radar net. So classified was the mission that the flight crew, i.e. pilot/co-pilot/navigator, were not allowed to pass into the cabin or talk to the electronic warfare crew during a mission.

The EC-47N was powered by Pratt & Whitney R-1830-92 engines. An engine change to the

One of the specialized versions of the Gooney Bird was the SC-47 air rescue variant that carried life rafts and rescue supplies. The observation blister just over the side numbers was particular to SC-47s. This SC-47B was from Detachment 6 based at Hamilton Field in 1946, and was painted Olive Drab and Medium Green 41, with Yellow Rescue markings. (Don Garrett Jr.)

P&W R-1830-90D engine led to a change in the designation to EC-47P, and a further upgrade to P&W R-2000-4 engines, plus updated ELINT equipment again led to a redesignation to the EC-47Q. EC-47Ns began deploying to South Vietnam during the buildup of 1965. They were assigned to the 460th Tactical Reconnaissance Wing based at Tan Son Nhut near Saigon, near Saigon. They were assigned to the 460th Tactical Reconnaissance Wing based at Tan Son Nhut near Saigon.

A very colorful SC-47B of the RCAF Maritime Command at Trenton RCAF Base in June of 1971. The aircraft was Silver and White, with International Orange fuselage and wing tip bands, and a Red and White engine cowl flash and fuselage cheat line. (Tom Brewer Collection)

The first Gooney Bird to have the designation of AC-47 was a radio monitoring aircraft of the Air Force Airways and Communication Service. These aircraft were quite colorful with their distinctive Day Glo Orange markings. AC-47s were used to monitor Soviet radar emissions. (Sidney Bremer)

with detachments at bases throughout South Vietnam and Thailand. The "Electric Goons" were operated throughout the Vietnam War by USAF, VNAF, Laotian, and Cambodian Air Force units. Most of the out-country missions were flown from Nakhon Phanom Royal Thai Air Base, supporting attack, search and rescue, and troops-in-contact strikes in the Barrel Roll area of northern Laos.

Fuselage Development

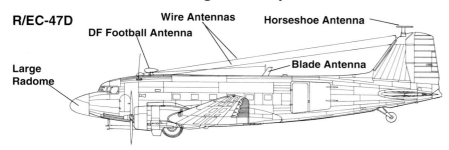

R/EC-47D

- Wire Antennas
- Horseshoe Antenna
- DF Football Antenna
- Blade Antenna
- Large Radome

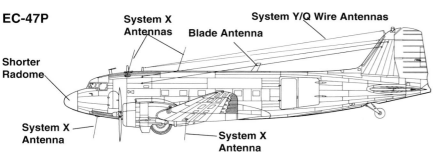

EC-47P

- System X Antennas
- System Y/Q Wire Antennas
- Blade Antenna
- Shorter Radome
- System X Antenna
- System X Antenna

The war in Vietnam saw the designation, AC-47 changed first to RC-47, then to EC-47. The mission of the VNAF EC-47s was to monitor Viet Cong radio traffic. This VNAF EC-47D sits outside the aircraft shelter at Clark Air Base during 1974. (David Menard)

This EC-47D of the Brazilian Air Force was returned to the U.S. after being phased out of active service. Although designated EC-47, the Brazilian aircraft did not possess the electronic monitoring equipment found in USAF aircraft. (Don Garrett Jr.)

A C-47A "Bullshit Bomber" or Psywar aircraft, on the ramp at Da Nang in December of 1966. The BS Bombers had a large speaker mounted in the rear cargo door, through which anti-communist messages were broadcast. (Tom Hansen)

7th Air Force airmen load flares into a C-47 BS Bomber at Phan Rang, South Vietnam. The BS Bombers also flew night forward air control and CANDLE flareship missions and were often escorted by AC-47 Spooky gunships. (USAF)

Antenna Array

C-47

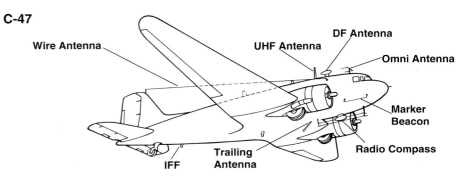

Wire Antenna · UHF Antenna · DF Antenna · Omni Antenna · Marker Beacon · Radio Compass · Trailing Antenna · IFF

EC-47P

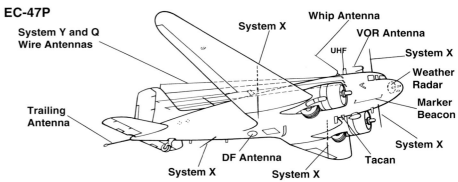

System Y and Q Wire Antennas · System X · Whip Antenna · VOR Antenna · UHF · System X · Weather Radar · Marker Beacon · System X · Trailing Antenna · DF Antenna · Tacan · System X · System X

An EC-47N "Electric Goon" from the 361st Tactical Electronic Warfare Squadron reveals System X antennas above and below the outer wing. The extended radome housed a weather avoidance radar. (Norm Taylor)

An EC-47P from the 361st TEWS at Phu Cat during 1971. This particular EC-47 has only two fuselage wire antennas. The EC-47P was basically an upgraded EC-47N with P&W R-I830-90D engines and improved electronics. (Norm Taylor)

In addition to the broadcast messages through the speaker horn, the C-47 BS Bombers dropped Cheu Hoi surrender/safe passage leaflets through a large chute on the underside of the starboard fuselage. (Tom Hansen)

An EC-47P assigned to the 361st Tactical Electronic Warfare Squadron/460th Tactical Reconnaissance Wing, undergoes engine maintenance at Phu Cat in September of 1970. This EC-47P has six wire antennas running from the sides of the vertical fin to posts on the fuselage top, in addition to numerous FM Command and other classified systems aerials. (Norm Taylor)

AC-47D Gunships

The AC-47D Gunship was a totally new breed of Gooney Bird. This one was mean and could shoot back! In 1963 the USAF held a conference to determine the best aircraft types to effectively defend the villages and hamlets in South Vietnam. Fighter aircraft were reasonably effective, but only during daylight hours, but Charlie always hit you at night and most of the fighter types couldn't put their ordnance on the target accurately enough if the enemy was "in the wire". What was needed was some type of aircraft that could fly low and slow, at night, and bring accurate fire to bear on the attacking VC.

An Air Force team adopted an old Second World War idea dreamed up by Colonel G. C. McDonald. His idea was to fly a pylon turn, with your weapons firing laterally or sideways. This would bring concentrated and accurate fire onto an enemy force from almost directly overhead. Captain Ron Terry headed the program to develop the side-firing weapons system using a C-47D as the gun platform. In late 1964 Terry's team installed a trio of General Electric SUU-11A/A Minigun pods in the fuselage of a standard C-47D. Sighting was accomplished through the use of a modified A-1 Skyraider gunsight mounted in the left cockpit window. The test results were amazing! Each pod could deliver 6,000 rounds per minute, for a total of 18,000 rounds per minute with all three guns firing! A one minute burst from all three guns could put a bullet in every foot of a football field, end to end and side to side! And it was accurate to within 100 feet of the friendlies!

Combat tests of the prototype gunship in South Vietnam were equal to the initial test results, only more so. So much so that the single gunship aircraft and crew were overwhelmed with requests for their fire support. A Stars and Stripes reporter nicknamed the gunship "Puff - The Magic Dragon" because of its awesome sight and roar at night, "it was like a dragon!" Because of the constant eerie night missions, the crews adopted the call sign of "Spooky." Air Force brass designated the "new" aircraft as an FC-47D for Fighter/Cargo! But the fighter jocks bitched up a storm and Air Force changed the designation to AC-47D for Attack/Cargo.

In early 1965, PACAF ordered an additional four gunships, but General Electric could not supply the mini-gun pods for the conversion. These four aircraft, also designated FC-47D, were modified at Clark AFB in the Philippines for the gunship role with eight to ten .30 caliber M-2 machine guns firing through holes cut in the fuselage side and door. They used the same Mk 20/Mod 0 gunsight as the minigun aircraft. Upon completion they were rushed to South Vietnam where they performed alongside the minigun equipped prototype. All five FC/AC-47Ds were assigned to the 4th Air Commando Squadron at Nha Trang. As GE caught up with minigun pod production in 1966, all the M-2 armed gunships were converted to miniguns. Although based at Nha Trang, like the EC-47s, the FC/AC-47Ds were rarely at "home plate", with detachments of single aircraft at forward bases throughout Vietnam.

By 1967 the minigun pods were being replaced by the GE MXU-470/A minigun module. The MXU-470/A module was specifically designed for the gunship mission. It used the same 7.62MM gatling gun, but it was now mounted directly to a vertical stand. This eliminated the problem of the ten minute reload time for gun pods. Plus the gun barrels were completely out in the open and kept much cooler, thus they lasted longer. Each FC/AC-47D also carried 45-60 flares, and at least 15,000 rounds of ammunition. They had UHF/VHF, and FM radios to talk to virtually anyone! The gunships were used as flareships, day and night forward air control aircraft, even as "escorts" for Psywar aircraft.

How effective were the AC-47 gunships? Air Force built forty-seven AC-47Ds, forty-one of

An EC-47Q from the 362nd TEWS on the ramp at Ubon RTAB in December of 1972. The EC-47Q had upgraded electronic equipment and was powered by P&W R-2000-4 engines. There are two large blade antennas under the rear fuselage. (Harley Copic)

Snuffy Smith was one of four C-47D trash haulers that were converted to the gunship configuration during 1965 by installing ten .30 caliber machine guns in the left side of the fuselage. The original designation for the gunships was FC-47D for Fighter-Cargo. (USAF)

which went to war in Southeast Asia. Twelve were shot down before the AC-47 mission became "Vietnamized" during 1969. The USAF AC-47Ds flew almost 5,000 missions. Old "Puff" defended 3,926 Vietnamese, Cambodian, and Laotian hamlets and villages from attack. Not one was overrun when a gunship was on the scene! The AC-47Ds are credited with between 50,000 and 75,000 casualties inflicted on VC or North Vietnamese troops.

The AC-47D was phased out of USAF service beginning in 1969. But the AC-47Ds soldiered on in the VNAF, Cambodian, and Laotian Air Forces. Following the end of the war in 1973, several found their way to units in both the Thai and Philippine Air Forces, again fighting communist insurgents. The constant upheaval in Central American countries such as El Salvador and Honduras saw a resurgence in the gunship concept. In 1984 the U.S. supplied El Salvador with at least four AC-47 aircraft armed with .50 caliber machine guns firing through the left side windows. In 1987, Project PEACE EMERALD saw eight C-47Ds modified at E-Systems to AC-47D for Columbia, complete with a Forward Looking Infrared system. It appears as though the AC-47 gunship might survive into the year 2,000, with turboprops and newer electronics.

(Right) Airman C.A. Shaw stands by the two four-gun batteries of .30 caliber machine guns that fired through holes cut in the rear cargo door. The FC-47Ds were assigned to the 4th Air Commando Squadron at Phan Rang during 1965. (C.A. Shaw)

The 3rd ACS Detachment parked in the revetments at Da Nang in 1967. The two gunship squadrons had Dets throughout South Vietnam at the height of the war, flying gunship support of troops in contact at night, as flareships and FACs, and as truck busters along the Ho Chi Minh Trail. (Larry Sutherland)

Members of the 3rd Special Operations Squadron pose by one of the later model AC-47Ds at Nha Trang during 1969. The "ghost" emblem on the nose symbolized the varied gunship mission. It carried a lantern in one hand for night flareship, and a lightning bolt in the other for the gunship mission. (Bill Platt)

This AC-47D was assigned to the base security flight at Udorn RTAB and shows at least 100 personnel, three trucks, and five artillery pieces as kill markings on the fuselage in White. AC-47s were replaced by AC-130 and AC-119 gunships in Vietnam during the early 1970s. (Colonel J. Ward Boyce)

A SUU-11A/A 7.62mm gatling gun pod was the initial armament of the FC/AC-47D gunship. The pods were later replaced by General Electric MXU-470 Minigun Modules. (USAF)

54

Super DC-3/C-117D

There were actually two completely different aircraft types designated the C-117. One was a more civilized C-47 type aircraft, while the other was a radically different development. The first C-117 was quite simply a C-47B that was outfitted with a more comfortable airliner type passenger compartment. Towards the end of the Second World War, the Army Air Force decided they wanted a more comfortable transport aircraft for use by the officer corps. As a result, Douglas received an order to build seventeen C-47Bs modified with a twenty-one seat airliner-style passenger compartment, complete with the small airliner-type entry door. These transport aircraft would be designated the C-117A, and were powered by Pratt and Whitney R-1830-90C engines rated at 1,200 horsepower, the same as that of the C-47B. C-117As were delivered in late 1944/early 1945 and eleven were later modified by removal of the two-stage supercharger and redesignated as C-117Bs. Following the end of the war several VC-47 staff transports were brought up to C-117B standards and designated as C-117C/VC-117C.

The C-117D was the military development of the Douglas Super DC-3. The Super DC-3 was a Douglas development to meet both airline requirements for a newer aircraft, and Federal Aviation Authority requirements which conceivably could ground the entire overage DC-3/C-47 fleet. The Super DC-3 fuselage was lengthened three feet three inches forward of the wing spar and, at the same time, the entire fuselage was strengthened. This "stretch" increased the seating capacity to thirty. Both the vertical and horizontal tail surfaces were also increased in size. The vertical fin was over a foot taller and more squared off, with a large fin fillet for added stability. The horizontal stabilizer was also increased in overall size and had the tips squared off.

The wing center section was unchanged, but the outer wing panels had a four degree sweep to the trailing edge and squared off wing tips. The squared tips reduced the wingspan almost five feet. The engine nacelles were completely redesigned to accept either the Pratt and

Fuselage Development

C-47

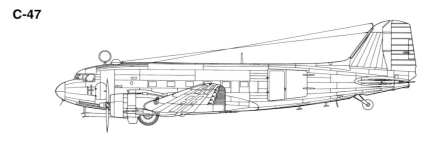

C-117D

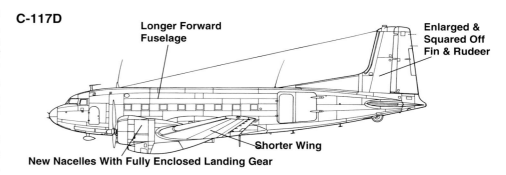

Longer Forward Fuselage

Enlarged & Squared Off Fin & Rudeer

Shorter Wing

New Nacelles With Fully Enclosed Landing Gear

The R4D-8 (C-117D) was a military adaptation of the Douglas Super DC-3. The R4D-8 was over three feet longer, with a much larger vertical fin and redesigned outer wing. It was powered by Wright R-1820 Cyclone engines. (Jim Sullivan)

55

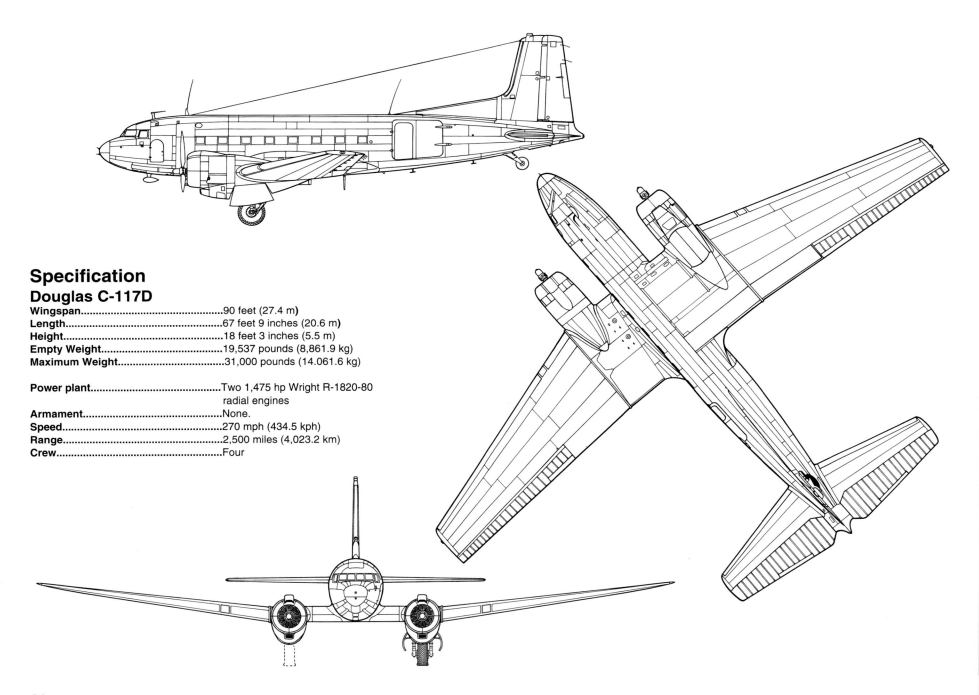

Specification
Douglas C-117D
Wingspan	90 feet (27.4 m)
Length	67 feet 9 inches (20.6 m)
Height	18 feet 3 inches (5.5 m)
Empty Weight	19,537 pounds (8,861.9 kg)
Maximum Weight	31,000 pounds (14.061.6 kg)
Power plant	Two 1,475 hp Wright R-1820-80 radial engines
Armament	None.
Speed	270 mph (434.5 kph)
Range	2,500 miles (4,023.2 km)
Crew	Four

Wing Development

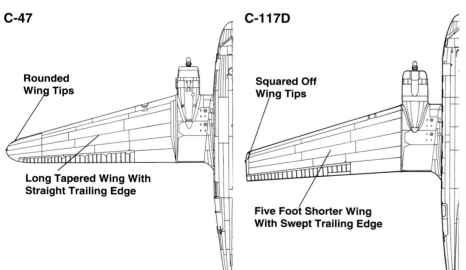

C-47

Rounded
Wing Tips

Long Tapered Wing With
Straight Trailing Edge

C-117D

Squared Off
Wing Tips

Five Foot Shorter Wing
With Swept Trailing Edge

A Navy R4D-8 from VT-29. All the R4D-8s were converted from earlier R4D-5, -6, and -7 airframes, which was much cheaper than buying new Convair C-131s. Douglas modified 100 airframes to the R4D-8 standard. (Bob Lawson)

Whitney 1,450 horsepower R-2000, or the Wright 1,475 horsepower R-1820. The landing gear was fully enclosed by a set of landing gear doors. Two standard aircraft, a DC-3 and a C-47, were modified to Super DC-3 standards. The first flight of the Super DC-3 came on 23 June 1949. Tests of the new design revealed a marked increase in all areas of the performance envelope. The maximum speed jumped to 270 mph, with the cruising speed up to 250 mph. But the airlines did not want a "converted" aircraft and opted to buy the all-new Convair-Liner.

Douglas then turned to the military. The U.S. Air Force was initially interested and began tests on the new aircraft, designating the Super DC-3 as the YC-129. This was later changed back to YC-47F. But the Air Force also decided in favor of the Convair design, which was standardized as the C-131. The U.S. Navy, however, was very interested in the design. During 1951, the original Super DC-3 prototype, the YC-129/YC-47F, was transferred to the Navy where it was designated as the R4D-8X. The Navy liked the overall airplane and its capabilities, especially its comparatively low cost as compared with the new Convair C-131.

Douglas received a contract to convert one hundred older R4D-5s, -6s, and -7s to the R4D-8 configuration. They would use the 1,475 horsepower Wright R-1820-80 engines. The fuel capacity was almost doubled to over 1,330 gallons. The weight of the R4D-8 naturally increased with the larger tail, enclosed landing gear and increased fuel capacity, with the

A Navy C-117D from the "Gecko Airways," a base flight unit at NAS Cubi Point, in the Philippines. The large cargo door was common to the C-47/C-117 type. The DOD adopted a new designator system in 1962 which saw the R4D-8 being redesignated as a C-117D. (P. Burgess)

A VC-117D from H&MS-27 at Marine Corps Air Station Cherry Point, North Carolina. It has a passenger door rather than the normal large cargo door. (Jim Sullivan)

empty weight of the new design now at 19,080 pounds and maximum weight increasing to almost 32,008 pounds. Although the fuel capacity doubled, the range, due to the increase in weight, only increased by one third, going from 2,150 miles to 3,050 miles.

In 1962, the DOD standardized the U.S. military designation system and the R4D-8 became the C-117D. Many C-117Ds were used for missions other than that of transport. The R4D-8T was a navigational and flight trainer, becoming the TC-117D, the R4D-8Z was a plush staff transport and was redesignated VC-117D, cold weather aircraft were R4D-8Ls which became LC-117Ds. The R4D-8/C-117D saw extensive use during the combat in Korea and Vietnam. *Trans Paddy Airways* was a C-117D assigned to the 3rd Marine Air Wing at Da Nang during 1967. Navy/Marine C-117Ds served in Vietnam in missions similar to USAF C/EC-47s. The last C-117D was retired in July of 1976. (Tom Hansen)

They were used as night drop and flareships in Korea, many of them wearing a distinctive Gloss Black paint on their undersurfaces. In Vietnam they were used almost exclusively as transports, although there were some used as electronic monitoring aircraft similar to the Air Force EC-47. The last C-117D was retired from active service in July of 1976.

A R4D-8L from VX-6 during 1969. It has an extended nose radome housing a weather avoidance radar. The aircraft was painted Silver and Navy Gray, with a Red tail, nose, and wing tips. (Don Garrett Jr.)